Operating within the law

A practical guide for surgeons and lawyers

By

Professor Bruce Campbell

Ken Callum

Nicholas A. Peacock

PUBLISHER

tfm Publishing Limited
Brimstree View
Kemberton
Nr. Shifnal
Shropshire
TF11 9LL

Tel: 01952 586408
Fax: 01952 587654
E-mail: nikki@tfmpublishing.co.uk
Web site: www.tfmpublishing.co.uk

Design and layout: Nikki Bramhill

First Edition   April 2001
ISBN 1 903378 05 2

Printed by Ebenezer Baylis & Son Ltd., The Trinity Press, London Road, Worcester, WR5 2JH. Tel: 01905 357979, Fax: 01905 354919.

C o n t e n t s

Operating within the law

A practical guide for surgeons and lawyers

CONTENTS

Page

Part II
Clinical Negligence - Legal Principles

Part III - Avoiding Medico-legal Problems

Page

Glossaries

Further information

Appendices

Surgeons in the United States have long regarded "malpractice suits" as an occupational hazard and just one of the regular frustrations of surgical practice. Not so in the United Kingdom, where medico-legal claims have only recently become commonplace. For most surgeons a law suit still provokes anger, depression, and a feeling of damaged professional pride: surgeons feel deeply threatened and lose sleep when a claim hangs over them. These reactions are due in no small measure to a lack of clear understanding about the medico-legal system. A primary aim of this book is to provide clear and concise explanations about all aspects of the medico-legal process for surgeons and other doctors. From the lawyer's perspective, some aspects of the health service are rather arcane, as are many details of surgical practice and surgeons' aspirations. Illuminating such issues for lawyers is an equal purpose of the book.

Surgeons interact with lawyers not only when they are sued, but also when they are asked to provide opinions as expert witnesses and occasionally in other capacities. They may provide explanations and reports which lawyers find difficult to understand - with regard not only to the way they are written, but also with regard to the point of view and general approach of the surgeon. We hope to narrow the gulf of mutual misunderstanding by explaining both the surgeon's and the lawyer's viewpoints on a variety of issues. The book includes separate **glossaries** of medical and legal terms which are in common use; which are important to understanding of the health service and the law; and which are specific to the text of some sections. Terms included in the glossaries are printed in bold type where they first appear in the text.

Sexual propriety always poses a dilemma when writing: continual use of he/she or s/he does not make for the easiest reading. We have opted for the use of "he" throughout the text for the sake of simplicity.

Professor Bruce Campbell
Ken Callum
Nicholas A. Peacock
15th January 2001.

PART I

Medico-legal Activity

A Changing Landscape

Increasing numbers of complaints and medico-legal proceedings against surgeons are affecting their morale, their culture, and their clinical practice. Combined with dramatic press coverage of "rogue" doctors, adverse medical events of any kind, and the National Health Service in general, the profession has good reason to feel besieged.

For the individual practitioner medico-legal **action** by a patient is the most damaging of all these influences, especially when he feels that he has done his best to care for the patient. Prevention of legal claims should therefore rank high in the training and practice of all doctors, and they also need to know the basic principles of handling medico-legal actions. This is something they do not have to do alone, and understanding the teamwork involved in dealing with complaints and legal proceedings is a great advantage.

When a patient suffers damage as a result of a medical accident or poor treatment then it is right that they should expect fair and appropriate compensation. However, many medico-legal claims concern adverse events which were recognised hazards of treatment, or which formed part of a generally unsatisfactory contact with a hospital service. Most can be avoided by clear, sympathetic communication, and dealt with more expeditiously if all records are thorough and lucid.

Patients increasingly expect their medical advisors to inform them in detail about the need for treatment, their choices, and what exactly would be involved. By contrast there is rather less enthusiasm for information about possible adverse outcomes, although there is usually a retrospective expectation that these should have been described beforehand, if by chance things do "go wrong". Information is also an important modern concept in the sense of "freedom of information" - the expectation that the patient should have full access to their medical records, but that confidentiality should be properly preserved at all times. Communication and record keeping will be recurring themes in this book, because they are the keys to avoiding and dealing with most medico-legal problems.

This section of the book will examine the recent increase in medico-legal activity and its general consequences.

C h a p t e r 1

The increase

in

medico-legal activity

Why measuring any increase is difficult

Until 1989 all claims against doctors (whether NHS or private, GP or consultant) were handled by the doctor's own **defence society**. Traditionally each defence society instructed its own firm of solicitors. In 1989 liability for all claims against hospital doctors in respect of NHS work was transferred to the Health Authority (now NHS Trust) by whom they were employed or engaged. There was no uniform national mechanism for dealing with these claims, nor of recording them, since each Health Authority/Trust was at liberty to instruct any firm of solicitors it chose. This changed in 1995 with the formation of the **National Health Service Litigation Authority (NHSLA)** which took charge of administering three different schemes:

❖ The **Clinical Negligence Scheme for Trusts (CNST)** - a voluntary scheme to indemnify Trusts against settlements above a chosen excess.

❖ The **Existing Liabilities Scheme (ELS)** - this funded all claims against NHS bodies for incidents prior to April 1995 and with total costs exceeding £10,000.

❖ The ex-RHA (Regional Health Authority) Liabilities Scheme - funding claims against hospitals managed directly by RHAs, such as the London Postgraduate Teaching Hospitals.

Solicitors were invited to tender for Health Authority/Trust work, which was then allocated to them by Region. Thus the claims work for all Health Authorities/Trusts in any Region (there are 18) is handled by one firm of solicitors, overseen by the NHSLA. Accordingly, the NHSLA is now able to manage more efficiently:

❖   the cost of litigation against hospital doctors;

❖   the size of claims paid out;

❖   specific legal issues as and when they arise.

The defence societies still deal with all claims against doctors in **primary care** and all claims in respect of private work by any doctor.

The variety of different organisations dealing with claims, combined with lack of a national database, and all the changes described above have made access to comprehensive information and assessment of trends very difficult. The water has been muddied still further by estimates of the cost to the NHS of negligence claims in the press, which have assumed that all outstanding claims will result in payment, when it is likely that the majority will not.

The best national figures

The most explicit figures have been published by Fenn et al [1] based on the database of the Oxfordshire Health Authority from 1974-1998. This database was substantial containing 902 active and 1993 closed clinical negligence cases. There was a steady increase in both new and closed claims, with an accelerating pace of change from the 1970s through to the late 1990s. Between 1990 and 1998 the number of closed claims doubled (55 versus 126 per annum respectively) with an average annual growth of 11%. During this period hospital activity increased by about 3.5% so Fenn et al [1] calculated the rise in the rate of closed cases per 1000 finished consultant episodes as 0.46 in 1990 and 0.81 in 1998 - an average increase of 7% per annum. Fenn et al [1] pointed out that this

7% increase in settled claims was indeed a substantial rate of growth, but not the "uncontrolled expansion" often perceived by the press and the medical profession.

There are good reasons to believe that these Oxfordshire data are representative. The district population (of 610,000 in 1998) has demographic features similar to the U.K. in general. In addition, comparison with figures from a sample of 61 English Trusts showed a rate of paid claims for 1998 similar to that in the Oxfordshire Health Authority [1].

Causes of the increase in medico-legal claims

To a large extent, the increase in medico-legal activity reflects general changes in the attitude of our society. *Accountability* is a fundamental theme - somebody must be responsible and must shoulder the blame when anything does not go exactly according to plan [2]. *Compensation* is another central issue - the idea that anybody suffering an adverse event should expect financial recompense (even when they have suffered no kind of financial loss).

There can be no argument that a doctor (or anyone else involved in patient care) should be fully "accountable" if a patient has suffered as a result of their poor performance or negligence, and that the patient should be properly compensated. However, many adverse events occur even when the standard of care has been entirely adequate, and the **outcome** was simply unexpected. *Expectations* contribute in a most important way to all medico-legal claims, and they are inextricably linked with *information*. A huge amount of information about medical issues is thrust at people by the press, television, and radio; and still more is available on the internet, in magazines, and in books, for those who want it. The information provided by the media tends to dwell on new advances and the possible achievements of modern medicine, which heightens expectation for treatment. This information is never counter-balanced (nor indeed seasoned much at all) by education about the limitations, possible **complications**, or cost effectiveness of

5

interventions. People are led to expect increasingly sophisticated treatments, often with unrealistic concepts not only of their potential benefit but also of their safety and availability.

Lawyers must inevitably bear some of the responsibility for the increase in medico-legal claims. This work forms a part of their livelihood and they are therefore keen to advise on any possible cases. Solicitors who specialise in medical negligence work are usually quick to recognise those cases which are groundless, but those with less special experience may pursue claims which are without merit (and may do so more slowly). There is a particular temptation to pursue such claims if the **claimant** is not liable for **costs**, and the legal aid system has been a significant factor both in the increasing number and increasing costs of claims initiated in recent years. Changes in the system of funding, and increasing specialisation among lawyers may well start to reverse these trends [3].

The **Legal Aid Board** has now been replaced by the **Legal Services Commission**, which funds claims by those who cannot afford to do so otherwise. **Legal Aid** (now renamed **public funding**) has been abolished for all **personal injury** claims except clinical negligence actions. Victims of road traffic accidents, accidents at work, and the like, who would formerly have received Legal Aid must now seek funding through a no-win no-fee agreement (technically a **conditional fee agreement**) whereby the lawyers can **claim** an uplift on their usual fee if the claim succeeds. For **clinical negligence** actions, patients may be publicly funded, but may only be represented by a firm of solicitors which is either a member of the clinical negligence panel or which has a clinical negligence public funding franchise. For either, the **solicitor** must be able to demonstrate actual experience and ability in clinical negligence litigation. It is proposed that public funding will eventually be withdrawn from clinical negligence claims.

In pursuing groundless claims lawyers have been aided and abetted by the doctors on whom they have depended for **expert** opinions. In this respect some members of the medical profession are guilty of fuelling the increase in litigation and risk censure from their colleagues for substandard or suspect work in their capacity as experts. Some may simply be working outside their field of expertise.

Other ways for patients to seek redress

Over the last two or three decades only 30-40% of medico-legal claims have resulted in settlement [1,2] and the proportion seems to have declined in recent years. This means that the majority of claims are found to be groundless, and the patient (or their relatives) might better have pursued their grievance in other ways. Quite apart from a specific misunderstanding that "things going wrong" are often not due to negligence, there is a more general misconception that approaching a lawyer is the best way of seeking redress for any medical mishap.

Simply asking for an explanation or writing a letter of complaint in the first instance may well be the most constructive approach. However, both leave room for the suspicion that there could be a "cover-up" because the matter is being dealt with internally. This suspicion is particularly understandable if the patient and their relatives have already experienced poor communication, or an arrogant, patronising manner from those dealing with them. In these circumstances a lawyer may seem the best "outsider" to ask for help, without clear consideration of whether negligence really has played a part in the problem.

A legal avenue is also the most obvious route for the patient whose main aim is financial compensation. By contrast, it is not the best option for a patient or relatives who simply want a full explanation of what has gone on; who want to see those responsible educated or disciplined; or who genuinely want to ensure that "it can't happen again" by seeing some kind of change in the system of care.

The complaints system within the NHS is now highly developed and is described in detail in Chapter 15.

References

1. Fenn P, Diacon S, Gray A, Hodges R, Rickman N. Current cost of medical negligence in NHS hospitals: analysis of claims database. *BMJ* 2000; 320: 1567-71.

2. Palmer R. Medical negligence - causes, trends and lessons. *Health Care Risk Report* 1998 (October); 1-2.

3. Simons D. Medical negligence claims - view from the patient's lawyer. *Journal of the Medical Defence Union* 1999; 15: 11-2.

Chapter 2

The effect of medico-legal pressures on surgeons and their practice:

lessons from the United States

The effects of litigation on surgical practice are best seen in the USA, where the crescendo of medico-legal activity preceded that in the UK, and where litigation continues to be much commoner. There, too, the same fundamental problems apply, with little relationship between "malpractice" and medical error; and failure of communication at the heart of many claims [1].

Perhaps the most tangible result of litigation in the USA has been in the documentation of consent, with consent forms listing every kind of possible adverse outcome. Audio taping what patients are told, and video recording of procedures are other means of trying to ensure that records exist which will help in the **defence** of malpractice suits.

Less tangible, but hugely important, has been the burgeoning practice of "defensive medicine" - performing both non-invasive and invasive tests in excess of any sensible clinical need, and with a view to avoiding litigation or providing a robust defence. Other manifestations of defensive medicine are the slow pace of operating by many American surgeons, and the degree of supervision of all trainees, which contrasts with traditional practice in the United Kingdom. The inexorable move towards these working patterns will affect clinical throughput, the cost of services, and the preparation of trainees for mature, independent clinical practice when they are appointed to consultant posts.

The setting up of the **National Practice Data Bank (NPDB)** is another result of widespread litigation in the USA. This lists all practitioners for whom "malpractice" payments have been made. Its original aim was to restrict movement of substandard doctors from one state to another, but the system has many problems [1]:

❖ reporting by different hospitals is very variable (many never file reports);

❖ there is no differentiation between minuscule payments (made for a variety of reasons) and major settlements for serious negligence;

❖ there may be more than one "entry" on the system for a doctor relating to the same clinical incident;

❖ nearly 20% of doctors in the USA are currently listed on the NPDB (including some trainees).

Regular enquiries are made from the NPDB when appointing or re-accrediting staff, so doctors are subject to regular scrutiny based on their past medico-legal record. In addition to this there are now effective information links between the licensing boards of different states, which "track" doctors who have been subject to malpractice settlements. Moves along these lines have become inevitable in the United Kingdom since the case of Mr. Richard Neale who worked in the United Kingdom for several years before being found guilty of professional misconduct by the **GMC**, despite having been previously censured by the authorities in Canada.

The huge cost of medico-legal activity in the United States is reflected in enormous premiums for indemnity insurance. These form a very significant and essential annual expenditure for doctors, which needs, in turn, to be covered by the level of their charges to patients, and the number of procedures they undertake. The latter helps to fuel a vicious circle of "overtreatment" and medico-legal activity in the USA (and some other countries) when viewed through the eyes of surgeons working in the cash limited NHS system.

10

The least tangible effect of litigation is on the attitude and culture of surgeons in the USA, who not only practice defensively, but who generally regard litigation more as a normal part of "doing business" than their peers in the UK. Two small consolations exist. First, the UK has by no means caught up with the USA in its volume and culture of litigation. Second, surgeons are no longer the group most often sued in the USA - that dubious lead is now held by physicians both in secondary and primary care.

Reference

1.   Fischer JE. The effect of litigation on surgical practice in the USA. *Br J Surg* 2000; 87: 833-4.

Chapter 3

The cost

of

litigation

The most publicised sums of money associated with medico-legal actions are the huge settlements which are made in occasional cases. Very large payments are most frequent for obstetrics, relating to claims for brain damaged babies following birth asphyxia. An acute Trust with one million pounds turnover will typically have one claim for a brain damaged baby each year [1]. Most payments are for much smaller sums of money. All these settlements represent only a proportion of the total legal costs of claims, the majority of which are never settled, but all of which require investigation, and many require the costs of legal defence. Added to these are the "hidden" costs of that part of risk management activity aimed solely at avoiding litigation; the salaries of those providing "in house" legal services; and the additional work involved in practising "defensive medicine".

Fenn et al [2] have calculated an average payment per claim closed during 1994-8 by the Oxfordshire Health Authority of £18,092, with 0.21 closed claims per 1,000 **finished consultant episodes**. This represented a mean cost of £5.24 per finished consultant episode over all their clinical activity. Extrapolating these data to the NHS as a whole gives a mean prediction of £61 million per annum cost for claims (based on 11.53 million finished consultant episodes during 1997-98). In addition to this are the defence costs of claims which were not closed (estimated at £2.00 per finished consultant episode) which produce a predicted £23 million expenditure. In total, therefore, the cost to the NHS in England of defending and settling clinical negligence claims for 1998 probably amounted to some £84 million (predicted range £48 million to £130 million).

It is important to recognise the difference between the £84 million estimate for costs of medico-legal claims calculated by Fenn et al [2] and the much higher figure from the National Audit Office which has been cited in the press. A figure of £2.8 billion has been publicised as the "bill to be faced" by the NHS [3], but this represents the total cost of all open claims, only a minority of which are likely to result in payment. In addition, any payments may be spread out over many years. Throughout all the discussion of numbers of claims and costs to the NHS, it should be remembered that substantial costs are still borne by the defence organisations, who continue to indemnify all doctors practising privately, and doctors working in primary care.

The figures for England, and for the NHS, contrast with an estimated $80-100 billion as the annual medico-legal expenditure for the United States [4].

Figures 1 and 2 show the breakdown of claims settled by the Medical Defence Union during 1990-8 in secondary care: these claims relate largely to the private (non-NHS sector) but include some NHS claims initiated before 1990.

Figure 1.*

UK Settled Surgical Claims 1990 to 1998
Number of Claims

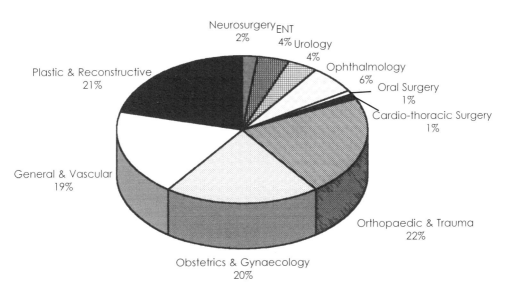

*Reproduced with the kind permission of The Medical Defence Union.
The Journal of the MDU, November 2000.

Figure 2.*

UK Settled Surgical Claims 1990 to 1998
Cost of Claims

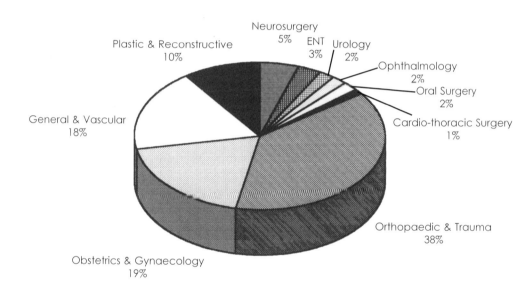

References

1. Capstick B. Incident reporting and claims analysis. *Clinical Risk* 1995; 1: 165-7.
2. Fenn P, Diacon S, Gray A, Hodges R, Rickman N. Current cost of medical negligence in NHS hospitals: analysis of claims database. *BMJ* 2000; 320: 1567-71.
3. Toynbee P. An arm and a leg. *Guardian* 1999. June 25.
4. Fischer JE. The effect of litigation on surgical practice in the USA. *Br J Surg* 2000; 87: 833-4.

C h a p t e r   4

The impact

of the

Human Rights Act 1998

On 2nd October 2000 the Human Rights Act 1998 came into force. The Act concerns the acts and omissions of public authorities (which include NHS Trusts, Health Authorities, and doctors treating NHS patients. There is debate, if not doubt, about whether it includes doctors treating private patients). Public authorities are required not to act in a way which is inconsistent with any of the rights guaranteed in the **European Convention on Human Rights** ("the Convention"). Whilst the mechanics are probably of interest to lawyers only, the effect of the Act is to enable litigants to rely on the various articles of the Convention in domestic courts (whereas previously such points could only be raised in the European Court of Human Rights after exhausting the domestic remedies available). Suffice it to say that UK courts are now obliged to take into account the Convention, and any relevant European case law, when determining the case before them.

The following Convention rights and articles will be of most interest to healthcare providers. What is worth bearing in mind is that, whilst the terms of the Articles themselves may appear clear and obvious, they have been developed by European case-law, often beyond what even the most imaginative lawyer might have thought possible:

Article 2 - Right to life

1. *Everyone's right to life shall be protected by law. No one shall be deprived of his life intentionally save in the execution of a sentence of a court following his conviction of a crime for which this penalty is provided by law.*

2. *Deprivation of life shall not be regarded as inflicted in contravention of this article when it results from the use of force, which is no more than absolutely necessary:*

   (a) *in defence of any person from unlawful violence;*

   (b) *in order to effect a lawful arrest or to prevent the escape of a person lawfully detained;*

   (c) *in action lawfully taken for the purpose of quelling a riot or insurrection.*

Article 2 is an absolute right and can never be derogated from (i.e. opted out of). It may have a considerable impact on UK medical law, because European case law has developed the principle that the concept that "everyone's right to life shall be protected by law" enjoins the State not only to refrain from taking a person's life "intentionally" but also to take appropriate steps to safeguard life [1]. It is possible (though academic opinion is divided) to argue that the obligation in Article 2 can be extended to include the obligation to make adequate provision for medical care in all cases where the right to life of a patient would otherwise be endangered. This would of course include every surgical operation. There is likely to be argument about whether "adequate" means the same as "reasonable". To date these arguments have not been extensively raised, still less resolved, in Europe.

Article 2 will also be raised in UK courts in the context of: abortion; enforced treatment; prolonging and withdrawing treatment in respect of patients who cannot consent.

Article 3 - Prohibition of torture, and of inhuman or degrading treatment or punishment

No one shall be subjected to torture or to inhuman or degrading treatment or punishment.

Again this is an absolute right and can never be derogated from. It has been held in Europe that forcible medical treatment and forced feeding could not be categorised as inhuman or degrading where they were therapeutically necessary [2]. However, the Court had to be satisfied that medical necessity had been convincingly shown to exist. In one case the European Commission on Human Rights decided that it "does not exclude that a lack of proper medical care in a case where someone is suffering from a serious illness could in certain circumstances amount to treatment contrary to Article 3" [3]. Experimental treatment may amount to inhuman treatment in the absence of consent, but would be inhuman only if it reaches a certain stage of gravity.

Article 2 and Article 3 are likely to be raised in conjunction with each other in medical cases in the future. Article 3 may be raised in the context of: understaffed nursing wards which lead to patients being unable to visit the toilet in time; patients being left on trolleys in corridors for long periods.

Article 8 - Right to respect for private and family life, home and correspondence

1. *Everyone has the right to respect for his private and family life, his home and his correspondence.*

2. *There shall be no interference by a public authority with the exercise of this right except such as is in accordance with the law and is necessary in a democratic society in the interests of national security, public safety or the economic well-being of the country, for*

19

the prevention of disorder or crime, for the protection of health or morals, or for the protection of the rights and freedoms of others.

Immediately it can be seen (from section 2) that this is a qualified right. Article 8 has been raised in European cases in the context of medical records. In one case [4] the Applicant had made a claim for compensation from the Social Insurance Office arising from a back injury at work. The Office requested her medical records (without her consent) from the head of the clinic who had treated her for a longstanding back condition. The records suggested that an abortion had been performed due to the back condition, making no reference to the accident at work (the abortion being four years later than the accident) and the Office rejected the claim. The Court held that there had been an interference with her right under Article 8 but that the interference was justified since it served the legitimate aim of protection of the economic well-being of the country. Importantly, the Court indicated that the Applicant had not waived her right to respect for her private life by submitting a claim for compensation. The ramifications of this are potentially enormous.

Impact on domestic law

In civil (ie, non-criminal) cases the Convention has had limited impact on the UK Courts, which have given strongly worded warnings to lawyers not to raise useless human rights arguments and enjoined judges to treat such arguments "robustly" [5] (judicial code for "with contempt"). Whether these suggestions will have an impact remains to be seen - the really interesting issues which may be affected by the European Convention on Human Rights have barely been raised in Europe to date. These are indeed interesting times...

References

1. Naddaf v Germany 50 DR 259.
2. Herczegfalvy v Austria (1992) 15 EHRR 437.
3. Tanko v Finland (1994) DR 77-A.
4. MS v Sweden (1999) 28 EHRR 313.
5. Daniels v Walker [2000] 1 WLR 1382, CA.

Further Reading*

1. McLean S. Old law, new medicine: medical ethics and human rights. Rivers Oram Press 1999.
2. Duffy P, Grosz S, Beatson J, Sedley, Eds. Human Rights: the 1998 Act and the European Convention. Sweet and Maxwell 1999.
3. Clayton R, Tomlinson H, George C. The law of Human Rights. Oxford University Press 2000.
4. Harris DJ, O'Boyle M, Warbrick C. Law of the European Convention on Human Rights, 2nd Ed. Butterworths Law 2000.
5. Wadham J, Mountfield H. Blackstone's guide to the Human Rights Act 1998, 2nd Ed. Blackstone Press 2000.
6. Starmer K, Klug F, Byrne I. Blacksone's Human Rights Digest. Blackstone Press 2000.
7. Wallington P. Blackstone's statutes on public law and human rights: 1999/2000, 9th Ed. Blackstone Press 1999.
8. Lord Lester of Herne Hill QC, Ed. Butterworths Human Rights cases. Butterworths Law 1998.
9. David, Harris M, Alistair, O'Boyle M. Cases and materials on the European Convention on Human Rights. Butterworths Law 2000.
10. Janis M, Key R, Bradley A. European Human Rights Law: text and materials, 2nd Ed. Oxford University Press, 2000.
11. Emmerson B, Ed. European Human Rights Law review - 1999. Sweet and Maxwell 2000.

* All books appearing in this list do not necessarily reflect an endorsement by the named authors or the publisher.

CHAPTER 4

PART II

Clinical Negligence

Legal Principles

Litigation against doctors is not a new concept, but there has been an explosion in the latter half of the twentieth century. Where once the occasional medical case would have been reported in a general series of law reports, there are now at least three series of law reports dedicated to medical cases. This has inevitably resulted in:

❖ increased public awareness of the possibility of suing a doctor;

❖ increased concern amongst doctors at the prospect of being sued and;

❖ as ever, an army of lawyers anxious to represent either side.

The principles which govern the legal relationship between a doctor and his patient, and the circumstances in which a claim against a doctor will succeed, are often misunderstood by doctors and patients (and lawyers) alike.

This chapter assumes the situation where a patient wishes to bring an action against a doctor (or healthcare provider) for **damages** in respect of the doctor's treatment of that patient. Lawyers now classify such actions as **clinical negligence** actions, rather than "medical negligence" actions. Doctors will readily understand the reason: "medical" negligence might be thought - though perhaps only by pedants - not to cover, e.g. "surgical" negligence. Strictly, the patient will commence **an action for personal injuries caused by clinical negligence**, reflecting the fact that clinical negligence actions are in fact a sub-group of a wider class of (personal injury) action.

Chapter 5

Anatomy

of a

legal claim

The duty of care

No-one can successfully **sue** a doctor and obtain an award of money unless he proves that the doctor owed him a duty to treat him. Accordingly the first question to be answered is whether such a duty exists at all.

This legal duty may in fact be imposed by two branches of law: (i) the **law of tort**, invariably its main sub-category, **negligence**, and/or (ii) the **law of contract**. A doctor treating a patient on the NHS will owe a tortious **duty of care** to his patient; a doctor treating a patient privately will also owe a contractual duty (of care) to his patient. Some lawyers become very (probably unnecessarily) excited about whether the duty in contract is in any way different in nature or scope from the duty in negligence. In practice a patient will usually bring a tortious (the adjective from tort) claim for negligence.

To whom does the doctor owe this duty of care?

The only answer is: to the patient, and no other. Doctors have recently been found by the courts not to owe a legal duty of care to the following:

❖ an applicant for employment where the doctor is employed by the prospective employer to carry out a preliminary health check [1]; and

- ❖ a victim of crime examined by a forensic medical examiner at the police station [2]; and

- ❖ the family of a deceased child patient; the victim (and her family) of a mentally ill patient on his release from hospital (see Palmer below).

(Note that this section concerns only the legal, and not the doctor's professional or ethical, duty.)

> Palmer v Tees Health Authority [1999] Lloyd's Rep Med 351, CA. In June 1994 a man named Armstrong abducted, assaulted and murdered Rosie, the claimant's daughter. Armstrong lived in the same street as the Palmers. It was alleged that he had a history of childhood sexual abuse and that from the age of 16 he had been diagnosed as being very disturbed. Between March 1992 and July 1994 he was under the care of the defendants as a psychiatric in-patient. When admitted to hospital in June 1993 he admitted that he had sexual feelings towards children and that a child would be murdered after his discharge. After discharge he remained as an outpatient. The claimant alleged that the defendants had failed to diagnose that there was a real, substantial and foreseeable risk of Armstrong committing sexual offences and assaults on children. Mrs Palmer's claim was struck out. On appeal, upholding the trial judge's decision, it was held that it was relevant to consider what steps could have been taken to avoid the danger. In this case, the danger involved the interposition of a third party, Armstrong, over whom the defendants had limited control. In addition, the victim, Rosie, was not identifiable in advance, so the defendants could not issue any warning.

Law or policy?

Frequently, in deciding whether a duty of care is owed at all, decisions are reached which are based on **policy grounds** rather than what the lay observer might consider as equity or justice (i.e. who "ought to" win). The usual justification by judges for any restriction on the existence or extent of a duty of care is the argument which lawyers label the **floodgates** argument: thus, if a duty of care is extended to cover such and such new situation, the floodgates will open and the courts will be awash with new litigation. It is a feature of our legal system that there is a constant antagonism between the need for reasonable certainty in the law and the flexibility of judge-made law to cater for novel situations. It is this interplay which gives rise to a constantly changing legal landscape which may appear frightening to lawyer and layman alike but which reflects no more than the society which creates it. In particular it has often been stated that the categories of negligence are never closed: the law will deal with each new factual situation as it arises.

*An example of the speed at which the law can evolve can be seen from the so-called **unwanted pregnancy** cases (in which a child is born after a failed sterilisation operation or after false information is given (or omitted) as to the potential for the child to be disabled). Over the last twenty years or so the law had developed so as to enable the parents of the child to claim damages for the cost of bringing up the "unwanted" child. These claims could include the cost of care, the cost of food, clothing, etc, the cost of school fees and could sometimes exceed £300,000 where the child was born healthy. (Where the child was born disabled, the awards could be worth millions of pounds.) In McFarlane v Tayside Health Board [1999] 3 WLR 1301, the House of Lords decided that, since a child brought both benefits and burdens to the parents, and the benefit could not be calculated in*

27

mere financial terms, the benefit should be set off in full against the (financial) burden. The effect is that, at least where a healthy child is born, the parents can claim only for the inconvenience of the pregnancy itself and for the immediate cost of equipment for the child when it is born ("the layette"), reducing the value of such claims to a fraction of their previous cost. The full ambit of this decision is now being tested in relation to the birth in such circumstances of a disabled child [3].

Having established that the doctor owes him a duty of care, the patient must then prove, to the court's satisfaction that the doctor was in **breach of duty** and that the breach **caused injury, loss and/or damage**. The various elements involved are considered below.

Burden and standard of proof

The concept of proof is mentioned above. It is worth pointing out at this early stage that, in any case of clinical negligence, the **burden of proving the case** lies fairly and squarely on the claimant at all times. The **defendant** does <u>not</u> have to disprove the claim. In addition, the **standard of proof** is no more than the **balance of probabilities**, i.e. whether something is more likely than not to have occurred. This is different both from criminal cases (which require proof beyond reasonable doubt) and from what doctors, as trained scientists, recognise as proof.

Difficulties with the burden and standard of proof in cases where there has been an adverse outcome but no-one knows when or precisely how a mistake was made has led some claimants to seek to rely on a doctrine called "***res ipsa loquitur***" (literally "*the thing speaks for itself*" in Latin). Thus it has been argued that the mere fact that the particular adverse outcome in question occurred is suggestive of, or "proof" of, negligence. Whilst this doctrine, which lawyers now regard as a tool of **evidence** rather than a matter of strict legal principle, may apply at a very basic level in very obvious cases (eg, cutting off the wrong arm, leaving your watch in the patient's abdomen after an operation), the courts now take the strong view that the doctrine is of no real use in the majority of cases of alleged clinical negligence [4].

Breach of duty

Whether the duty of care is owed pursuant to a contract or is imposed by the law of negligence, the nature of the duty is, broadly speaking, the same: to treat the patient with **reasonable skill and care**. (A contract will usually be deemed to include an **implied term** to this effect; an express contractual term may go somewhat further). For all practical purposes the law does not generally distinguish between an act and an omission to act.

Having decided that the doctor does owe a duty to treat the patient with reasonable skill and care, the next issue to consider is whether the doctor's performance has come up to standard. Whereas in other areas of law, for example road traffic claims, this is usually a relatively simple matter to determine (the standard of care in road traffic accidents is that of the ordinary prudent driver), a different test applies where clinical negligence (and indeed professional negligence in general, including architects, surveyors, lawyers, etc.) is alleged.

A doctor breaches his duty to the patient if he fails to treat the patient with reasonable skill and care. However, a doctor is not guilty of negligence if he acts (or omits to act) in accordance with a practice accepted as proper by a responsible (or respectable or reasonable) body of medical opinion skilled in the relevant discipline (the "Bolam test"). In addition, that body of opinion must stand up to logical analysis (the "Bolitho gloss"). The Bolam test has been upheld by the House of Lords on no less than four occasions [5] and has been held to be the standard which applies to diagnosis and treatment as well as disclosure of risk.

29

*Although the case gave its name to the fundamental principle which governs the standard not just of doctors but all professionals, the facts of <u>Bolam v Friern Hospital Management Committee</u> [1957] 2 All ER 118 are relatively unimportant. The case, heard in 1954, involved a plaintiff who was suffering from mental illness and who was advised to undergo **electro-convulsive therapy**. He was not warned of the (very small) risk of fracture. During treatment he sustained dislocated hip joints and fractures of the pelvis on each side. There were different schools of thought within the profession as to the use of relaxant drugs and as to manual control during treatment. The case was heard by a jury (a practice since abolished in this type of case), who were directed by the judge in the terms set out above. The jury found for the defendants.*

In <u>Bolitho</u> [6] (the facts of which are set out on page 35) courts were encouraged (or, according to some lawyers, reminded) to subject the experts' views to logical analysis. This is not a new proposition:

<u>Hucks v Cole</u> [1993] 4 Med LR 393, CA. This case was in fact decided in 1968. The plaintiff was expecting her first child in October 1963. She found a septic spot on her ring finger which she treated herself with a Kaolin poultice. She showed her GP, the defendant, the spot a few days later. He gave no treatment, took no swab and did not tell the maternity hospital about it. The plaintiff was then admitted to the maternity hospital and had a baby girl. The next day a nurse noticed the septic spot and a further spot on the plaintiff's toe. On the following day the defendant visited, took a swab and prescribed a

five-day course of tetracycline, an antibiotic. The pathology report on the swab reported a number of organisms and indicated that penicillin would kill one of them but that tetracycline would have no effect on another. The defendant persisted with tetracycline for the full course, at the end of which the septic spots were not completely healed. The defendant did not place the plaintiff on penicillin and she became seriously ill with fulminating septicaemia. At trial, the experts disagreed as to the correct course of action. The trial judge found that the defendant was not negligent until the end of the course of tetracycline, after which he should have prescribed an antibiotic to get rid of the virulent organism. The Court of Appeal upheld this finding, indicating that the pathology report should have rung an alarm bell for every practitioner. The Court drew attention to the perceived lacuna in this case between what was done and what should have been done, holding that courts should examine such lacunae anxiously in every case to determine whether they were reasonable in the light of current medical knowledge.

Courts have since shown themselves willing to examine these lacunae, rejecting the views of defendants' experts on, for example, whether cytology screeners should have referred slides to a checker and/or pathologist where they were not sure that the slide was negative [7] and, in the following case, whether a general practitioner should have referred a patient to hospital after a fall:

Marriott v West Midlands Health Authority [1999] Lloyd's Rep Med 23, CA. In October 1984 the claimant fell downstairs at home: he suffered a head injury and was unconscious for 20-30 minutes. He was admitted to the first defendant's hospital by ambulance and discharged next day. His condition did not improve and one week later the third defendant, a GP, was called. The GP was informed of the claimant's condition and examined him. Neurological tests revealed no abnormality. The GP told the claimant's wife to contact him if his condition did not improve. Four days later the claimant's condition suddenly deteriorated and, unconscious, he was returned to hospital. He had sustained a massive left **extradural haematoma**. *At operation a linear fracture of the skull was discovered. The claimant was left severely disabled. He claimed that the GP negligently failed to realise the seriousness of his injury and to refer him to hospital. The GP's expert witness gave evidence that either re-admission or observation at home would be reasonable responses. The claimant's expert said that a GP in these circumstances should refer to hospital. The judge found that the only prudent course would have been to refer the claimant to hospital. Both experts indicated that they had discussed this case with their partners, who agreed. On appeal by the GP it was held that the judge was entitled to subject a body of opinion to analysis to see whether it could be regarded as reasonable and the appeal was dismissed.*

It is not the case, despite some media reports, that the Bolam test has been recently eroded. It will be rare that a court finds itself able to reject the views of eminent doctors as illogical, particularly where they demonstrate that they have taken into account the relative risks of treatment/failure to treat. However, a court will still be able to reject expert evidence with which it disagrees and, subject to the Bolam test, choose between competing expert views.

Not all adverse outcomes are the result of a doctor's mistake, let alone a negligent breach of duty. It is probably not helpful, however, to talk of "accident", "mistake" or "mere error of judgement" (not that this has dissuaded some courts from doing so). The only relevant test is: **did the doctor treat the patient with reasonable skill and care according to the <u>Bolam</u> test** (and did that cause the claimant's injury)? Any other formulation of the test required will probably lead to more confusion than clarification. A proper exploration of the circumstances in which a doctor treats (or omits to treat) the patient according to this test will (or should) take into account all the possible explanations of the adverse outcome.

Seniority of doctor

Somewhere within these principles the law must accept that there are different levels of doctors practising medicine. What is expected of a house officer will not be what is expected of a specialised consultant. Curiously, the law has struggled to formulate the principles which govern the standard by which different grades of doctor are to be judged [8] (it being easy to slip into the trap that a **junior doctor** may simply rely on his or her inexperience as a defence). However, in practice, the first relevant question to ask (and answer) is whether any doctor was appropriately qualified and experienced to undertake the procedure (or make the diagnosis or give the advice, etc) at all. A less experienced doctor will discharge his duty by seeking the advice, at the appropriate time, of a more experienced colleague. If the junior doctor should never have attempted to undertake a particular procedure, the negligence is not usually his, but rather his consultant's (or the system's) for allowing him to do so.

Good Samaritans

Finally, doctors are always anxious to know what duty they owe as passers-by in an emergency. The position is simple: a doctor who is merely present at an emergency (other than on duty) has no legal duty to intervene at all. If, however, a doctor chooses to intervene in such circumstances, his standard of care will be judged according to the Bolam test. Thus a General Practitioner would be expected to achieve the standard of the reasonably competent General Practitioner. A Consultant Orthopaedic Surgeon would be expected to achieve the standard of the reasonably competent Consultant Orthopaedic Surgeon. No doubt the Court would be sympathetic to the exigencies of the particular situation.

Causation

Few topics are more likely to start doctors and lawyers foaming at the mouth in desperation as the topic of **causation**. This is sometimes because doctors do not understand the legal test(s) involved and more often because lawyers do not understand the medicine involved (or sometimes, dare one say it, the legal test(s) involved!). The legal principles are in fact relatively easy to state, if not to apply.

The claimant must prove that the breach of duty he alleges caused the injury of which he complains. At the risk of repetition, the standard of proof is only the balance of probabilities. However negligently the doctor has acted (or omitted to act), the claimant will not obtain anything other than a moral victory without proof that the negligence caused him damage.

At its most basic, "causation" involves asking the simple question: **"But for the doctor's negligence, would the claimant have suffered the damage of which he or she now complains?"** (the "but for" test). If the claimant would have suffered exactly the same injury, loss and/or damage as he now complains about, his claim will fail (no matter how gross or obvious any breach of duty may be). The claimant may be able to interest the GMC in his case, but not a court. It is always for the claimant to prove his case on causation (and not for the defendant to disprove it).

Often, of course, this question is extraordinarily difficult for experts to answer factually, which is usually the point in the case where the lawyers smile smugly and point out that this is precisely why they instructed an expert in the first place.

Hypothetical causation

Sometimes one simply does not know what would have happened but for the negligence because, for example, the doctor who should have attended does not do so. In such cases (called **hypothetical causation** cases by lawyers) the claimant will succeed if he can show that either: (i) the relevant doctor would in fact have taken the requisite action to avoid the claimant's injury or; (ii) the proper discharge of that doctor's duty would have involved taking the requisite action. The latter scenario is now to be assessed according to the <u>Bolam</u> test.

> *<u>Bolitho v City & Hackney Health Authority</u> [1998] AC 232, HL. In December 1983 Patrick Bolitho (then aged 2) underwent an operation to correct a condition of patent **ductus arteriosis**. On 11th January 1984 he was admitted to St Bartholomew's Hospital suffering from acute croup. The following morning his condition had deteriorated and he was having difficulty in breathing. On January 13th he appeared to be cyanosed although he recovered quickly and was discharged on January 15th. That night he was restless and was readmitted to hospital the next day. His respiration rate was high with chest wall recession, which increased during the evening. The following morning he was better although there was reduced air entry on one side. He was examined by a consultant but Patrick's condition gave no special cause for concern. At about 12.40 pm Sister Sallabank asked the senior paediatric registrar, Dr Horn,*

to see Patrick straight away. She said she would attend as soon as possible. When the sister returned to Patrick, he was walking about and looked pink. A nurse remained with him. At about 2pm the nurse called Sister Sallabank back - Patrick had developed respiratory difficulty. Sister Sallabank called Dr Horn, who told her that she was on afternoon clinic and had asked a Dr Rogers to come in her place. Meanwhile Sister Sallabank was told that Patrick was pink again. Dr Rogers did not attend because her bleep was not working. At abut 2.30 pm Patrick, while retaining his colour, became agitated and started to cry. The nurse left a colleague with Patrick and reported to Sister Sallabank, who bleeped the doctors. The nurse set off the emergency buzzer while Sister Sallabank was on the telephone. A call was sent out for the crash team. Patrick had collapsed because he was unable to breathe. He suffered a cardiac arrest and severe brain damage as a consequence.

The Trial Judge found that the two attacks had occurred because a gobbet of mucus had obstructed Patrick's bronchial air passages and impaired his ability to breathe until he coughed. It was agreed that Dr Horn had been negligent in not attending when summoned by Sister Sallabank. The Plaintiff's case was that Patrick should have been **intubated** after the first (and certainly after the second) attack. The Defendant's expert stated that intubating Patrick was not necessary or desirable but conceded that intubation would, on balance, have averted his collapse. Dr Horn stated in evidence that she *would not have intubated. The Trial Judge held that Patrick had not proved that any competent doctor in the position of Dr Horn would have intubated him before his collapse.*

Patrick appealed. The House of Lords held that a plaintiff could succeed in such cases (where a hypothetical question was involved) by proving either (1) that the relevant person would have taken the action necessary to avert harm or (2) that no reasonable doctor could have failed to have taken that action. As to (1) the trial judge will make a straightforward finding of fact on the evidence available; as to (2) the legal test to be applied is the Bolam test. Patrick Bolitho's claim failed because the trial judge found, as to (1), that Dr Horn would not in fact have intubated and, as to (2), that it would not have been negligent to fail to intubate.

However, the House of Lords added this gloss to the Bolam test: where a Bolam defence was raised, the court had to be satisfied that any expert opinion to the effect that a doctor would not have been negligent had a logical basis, which involves weighing up the relevant risks and benefits. It could not be said in this case that the Defendant's expert's view was illogical. Accordingly, Patrick failed on both of the two possibilities.

Some have argued that the Bolam test, which applies at a very different stage in establishing a cause of action (i.e. at the stage of proving a breach of duty), should play no part in determining causation. However, it is worth bearing in mind that this argument probably leads to the seductive (in favour of the claimant) but logically flawed conclusion that, in filling the evidential gap, what <u>would</u> have happened is what <u>should</u> have happened.

Adverse outcomes which have several possible causes

Sometimes there may be several possible causes of an adverse outcome, some (or one) of which may be negligent and some (or one) non-negligent. Where it is possible that a breach of duty has, judged cumulatively, contributed to the adverse outcome in some significant (though perhaps indefinable) way, claimants may argue that the breach of duty has **materially contributed** to the injury [9]. They may succeed; they may not (e.g. where the negligent cause is in fact of little consequence). However, where the breach of duty is but one cause amongst many, all of which could separately (note, not in combination) have caused the injury, the claimant will find it difficult if not impossible to prove that the breach of which he complains caused his injury.

> *Wilsher v Essex Area Health Authority [1988] 1 AC 1074, HL. The plaintiff was born prematurely and he was placed in a special baby care unit at a hospital managed by the defendant. If he was to survive, he required extra oxygen, to be administered into a catheter through the umbilical artery. A junior doctor mistakenly inserted the catheter into the umbilical vein. Neither he nor the senior registrar realised that x-rays showed the catheter in the vein, though both realised there was something wrong with the monitor readings. The senior registrar inserted another catheter, but into the same vein. The next day, it was realised that the plaintiff had been supersaturated with oxygen for 8-10 hours. The catheter was replaced by one in the artery, after which arterial blood oxygen levels were monitored and at times during the following weeks the levels were considered too high. The plaintiff*

developed retrolental fibroplasia (RLF). A likely cause, but not definite nor the only possible cause, was that too much oxygen had been administered within the first 30 hours or at a later stage. The trial judge found the defendant liable. On appeal the House of Lords held that where a number of different factors could separately have caused the RLF, the fact that RLF occurred after the unnecessary over-saturation with oxygen was not evidence, nor did it raise any presumption, that the excess oxygen caused the RLF and the trial judge had been wrong to find for the plaintiff.

Lawyers have recently been sent into a spin by the Court of Appeal, which suggested that a defendant who contributed to (rather than caused) an injury should only be liable up to the extent of his contribution (rather than, as had previously been thought, for the full extent of the damage) [10]. The House of Lords may comment on this in due course.

References

1. Kapfunde v Abbey National plc [1999] Lloyd's Rep Med 48, CA.
2. Re N [1999] Lloyd's Rep Med 257, CA.
3. See, eg: Rand v East Dorset Health Authority Lloyd's Rep Med 181.
4. Delaney v Southmead Health Authority [1995] 6 Med LR 355; Ratcliffe v Plymouth & Torbay Health Authority [1998] PIQR P170.
5. Whitehouse v Jordan [1981] 1 All ER 267, HL; Maynard v West Midlands Regional Health Authority [1984] 1 WLR 634, HL; Sidaway v Bethlem Royal Hospital Governors [1985] 1 All ER 643, HL; Bolitho v City & Hackney Health Authority [1988] AC 232, HL.
6. Bolitho v City & Hackney Health Authority [1988] AC 232, HL.
7. Penney, Palmer & Cannon v East Kent Health Authority [1999] Lloyd's Rep Med 123, CA.
8. eg, Wilsher (supra).
9. Bonnington Castings v Wardlaw [1956] AC 613; McGhee v National Coal Board [1973] 1 WLR 1.
10. Holtby v Brigham & Cowan (Hull) Ltd [2000] Lloyd's Rep Med 254, CA.

Chapter 6

Defences

Avoiding liability

So far the circumstances have been considered in which a court may be persuaded to find in favour of the patient. Doctors will be keen to know in what additional circumstances, if any, a court might be persuaded to find against the patient. Apart from simply disputing the alleged breach of duty and/or causation on the facts/evidence, there are a number of other, separate, legal defences open in clinical negligence cases.

Supervening cause

Sometimes it is possible to argue that the subsequent negligence of another person in fact caused the claimant's injury, for example, where a claimant is transferred to a different NHS Trust for treatment. Lawyers sometimes refer to this defence as a **supervening cause**, which "breaks the chain of causation". Sadly it is of little assistance in practice.

Limitation

More important, and well-known, is the defence that an action is **time-barred** according to the Limitation Act 1980. Most doctors will know that a claimant must bring his action within three years. But three years of what? In fact a claimant must start proceedings within three years of either (i) the date on which he suffered his injury (which may sometimes be months or years after his actual treatment) or (ii) the date on which he had sufficient knowledge of the elements of his claim to be able to start proceedings, whichever date is later. There are various elements which a claimant must "know" (the elements being defined in **section 14** of the Act) for these purposes, and even more reported cases to provide "assistance" to lawyers on this topic.

Even if a claimant starts his action late, he can attempt to persuade the court to disapply the time limit. **Section 33** of the Act sets out the circumstances in which the court, in its **discretion**, may do so. In the reported cases, so many claimants are allowed to continue notwithstanding the fact that they brought their action **out of time** that some lawyers now doubt whether the defence is available at all in any but the most exceptional cases. (In fairness, it should be said that courts usually allow claimants to continue where, for example, all the witnesses are still alive and the medical records are still preserved in full so that experts are nonetheless able to comment sensibly on the claim, in other words a fair trial is still possible [1]) It in the combination of sections 14 and 33 which allows courts to find in favour of patients who underwent treatment many years previously, for example:

> *Smith v Leicester Health Authority [1998] Lloyd's Rep Med 77, CA. In 1950 the claimant (aged 7) developed weakness in her right leg and occasional incontinence. In October 1952 an orthopaedic surgeon diagnosed spina bifida. In November 1953 an operation at Leicester General Hospital to straighten the right knee did not improve her condition. In August 1954 a **neurogenic** bladder dysfunction was diagnosed. In December 1954 a bladder neck excision was done. Her incontinence increased after that operation. X-rays taken in 1954 and 1955 showed enlargement of the spinal canal, not reported by the radiologist. If they had been reported, a **myelogram** would have disclosed the presence of a*

mass, which could have been removed with little or no risk of paralysis. In May 1957 a **laminectomy** revealed a **dermoid** cyst within the spinal cord, which was aspirated by a surgeon. The claimant had breathing difficulties, followed by tracheotomy but became tetraplegic as a result of the laminectomy operation. The cyst had caused the bladder and leg problems.

In December 1983 the claimant overheard a doctor to the effect that a "mistake had been made". In spring 1984 she was advised by the Spinal Injuries Association that limitation had long since expired. In July 1988 she saw a solicitor who indicated she might have a claim. Legal Aid was issued in March 1989. In November 1990 a favourable expert opinion was obtained. A writ was issued in May 1995. The relevant X-rays were not tracked down until 1995.

The trial judge gave judgment for the defendant: although the defendant had been negligent in failing to diagnose the true condition in 1954/5 and the negligence caused the claimant's tetraplegia, the claimant had the requisite knowledge of her injuries and it would be inequitable to disapply limitation provisions because the defendant would be prejudiced.

On appeal it was held that it was not reasonable for the claimant to seek expert advice prior to 1989, but the expert had not identified the one issue of negligence which could succeed (failure of radiologist to report enlargement of spinal canal) at that time. The claimant *would not have found out prior to 1995 that her condition was caused by that negligence. The defendant could not establish that the claimant had the requisite knowledge more than 3 years prior to proceedings. Further the judge erred in not disapplying the three year period in any event: the prejudice to the claimant (in not being able to continue with her claim) far outweighed the prejudice to the defendant (who would still be able to defend the action). (Note that this trial concerned the limitation issue alone; the final outcome of the claim is not known.)*

Contributory negligence

Finally a word or two should be included about **contributory negligence**. Section 1 of the Law Reform (Contributory Negligence) Act 1945 enables a court, where the damage claimed is attributable to negligence on the part of both the claimant and the defendant, to reduce the award of damages accordingly. This defence, though often raised by a defendant, is rarely invoked successfully. The reason in practice is that a claimant will usually be able to argue, in response to an allegation of contributory negligence against him, that the doctor was at further fault (e.g. failure to give sufficiently clear advice, failure to provide adequate follow-up, etc).

References

1. Eg, Farthing v North East Essex Health Authority [1998] Lloyd's Rep Med 37, CA.

Chapter 7

How to value

a

legal claim

From the claimant's point of view, this is the most important topic: "How much is my case worth?" Some awards in clinical negligence actions are regularly reported in the media as evidence of the breakdown of the health service, law and society because of their perceived size.

Some understanding of how courts arrive at a final figure is therefore probably important before commenting on the size of a particular award. It should be pointed out that the **remedies** which a claimant can obtain from a court are few. In the normal run of clinical negligence cases a claimant may want far more than the award of damages which the court can provide. A court cannot order a defendant to apologise, nor will an explanation necessarily be provided. Rarely a court may order an **injunction** (the remedy of choice in cases where a healthcare provider seeks the court's guidance on, e.g. the withdrawal of treatment from an incompetent patient) or make a **declaration.**

An **award of damages** (in a tortious or negligence action) seeks to put the claimant in the position he would have been in if the breach of duty had never been committed (or, in contract cases, as if the contract had been performed). This formulation is called the **measure of damages**.

In principle, in an action for personal injuries caused by clinical negligence, there are two possible elements to any award:

❖ damages for **pain, suffering and loss of amenity** (which lawyers call **general damages**);

❖ sometimes, though not always, damages to compensate the claimant for his **pecuniary or financial loss** (which lawyers call **special damages**).

General damages

The calculation of this element of the award is purely academic, for how could a court ever truly compensate a claimant for such injuries as, for example, the loss of an eye or the loss of a woman's fertility with a mere sum of money? Nonetheless, this element of the award comprises in principle not only the injury itself (pain and suffering), but the consequences on the patient's life in general (loss of amenity). In practice, lawyers estimate the likely award of general damages by using any or all of the following:

❖ published **Guidelines by the Judicial Studies Board** (currently in their 5th edition);

❖ **previously reported** cases disclosing similar injuries (recently the Court of Appeal has authorised an increase in awards of general damages over £10,000 [1]) and;

❖ guesswork (usually referred to by lawyers as experience).

Special damages

Special damages cover financial or pecuniary loss for two periods: (i) between the negligence and the trial (**past loss**) and; (ii) from the trial into the future (**future loss**). Bearing in mind that few awards of general damages will ever exceed £200,000 it is easy to see that the element of an award which guarantees media attention is in fact the level of special damages. These vary from the relatively small and mundane (the cost of travel to medical appointments; a few extra pairs of shoes each year) to the considerably more substantial (loss of earnings, cost of care, significant new accommodation requirements). In principle, all loss between the negligence and the trial is capable of precise calculation (and should be capable of a fairly high level of proof, e.g. receipts, invoices, wage slips, etc). Future loss becomes progressively more difficult to prove the dimmer the court's crystal ball becomes.

The size of an award will usually be dependant on how much financial loss the claimant will or is likely to suffer in the future (after the trial). Where, for example, a claimant requires 24-hour paid nursing care for life and will live for a further forty years, or where a high-earning professional who would have generated a substantial private income until his early seventies is negligently injured in his mid-thirties, suffering a substantial loss of earnings as a result, it will readily be seen that the defendant is going to need a very deep pocket indeed to compensate the claimant. In fact the law is not quite so stupid as to simply add up forty years' worth of claim and hand the whole lot over to the claimant there and then - the value of the claim is **discounted** to take into account the **accelerated receipt factor** and the law has developed a mechanism for the calculation of such awards [2]. The idea is that the claimant will invest his award so as to provide for his future expenditure. (This provoked some media interest when the House of Lords recently adopted a slightly lower percentage figure as the return on investment, producing higher awards for future loss [3]).

Are awards in clinical negligence claims too high?

Possibly, but, firstly, they are not as high as in the US and will never be so long as lawyers are not entitled to a slice of the damages as their payment and also so long as judges, not juries, determine the level of award. Secondly, most doctors will take the view that, if the victim of an accident at work or the innocent victim of careless driving can sue, the victim of clinical negligence (if proved) is no less entitled to compensation.

References

1. Heil v Rankin [2000] 2 WLR 1173, CA.
2. See the Ogden Tables, set out in Facts & Figures (a Professional Negligence Bar Association publication) each year since 1997.
3. Wells v Wells [1999] 1 AC, HL.

Further Reading

1. Minns T. **Quantum** in medical negligence. Sweet and Maxwell 1998.
2. Buchan A, Langstaff B. Schedules of special damages. Butterworths Law 1999.
3. The Judicial Studies Board. Guidelines for the assessment of general damages in personal injury cases, 5th Ed. Blackstone Press 2000.
4. McGregor H. McGregor on damages, 16th Ed. Sweet and Maxwell 2000.

* All books appearing in this list do not necessarily reflect an endorsement by the named authors or the publisher.

Chapter 8

Legal procedure

The **procedural law** (the rules governing the management of the claim from commencement through to trial, including costs, enforcement of judgment and appeals) was overhauled with effect from 21st April 1999 by the **Civil Procedure Rules 1998** (CPR in legal shorthand). The guiding ethos behind the reformed procedure was to try to reduce the costs and duration of litigation.

The first matter which lawyers noticed after 21st April 1999 was that the **terminology** had changed. For example, where once we had **plaintiffs**, we now have **claimants**; where we had **discovery**, we now have **disclosure**; where we had **writs** and **summonses**, we now have **claim forms**. But the procedural landscape has changed far beyond the substitution of modern words for some old Latin-derived ones. Parties are now obliged to work together to achieve the satisfactory resolution of a claim. Indeed the Civil Procedure Rules go so far as to attempt to define (or at least point out some of the hallmarks of) justice. CPR Rule 1.1 states:

"(1) *These Rules are a new procedural code with the overriding objective of enabling the court to deal with cases justly.*

(2) *Dealing with a case justly includes, so far as is practicable:*
    (a) ensuring that the parties are on an equal footing;
    (b) saving expense;

(c) *dealing with the case in ways which are proportionate:*

    (i) to the amount of money involved;

    (ii) to the importance of the case;

    (iii) to the complexity of the issues; and

    (iv) to the financial position of each party;

(d) *ensuring that it is dealt with expeditiously and fairly; and*

(e) *allotting to it an appropriate share of the court's resources, while taking into account the need to allot resources to other cases."*

Just in case lawyers thought they might try to keep a low profile and hope that the new rules passed them by, CPR Rule 1.3 states:

"The parties are required to help the court to further the overriding objective."

There is much more **front-loading** of work in the new world - in other words much more work needs to be done by both sides before a claim is formally commenced in the courts. No longer can a patient write a **letter before action** (i.e. a letter intimating that a claim for damages will soon be formally commenced), wait a few weeks and then commence proceedings. Nor can a defendant keep all his cards close to his chest and ambush the claimant at the trial. We now have the **Pre-Action Protocol for the Resolution of Clinical Disputes**, which sets out a timetable for patients and healthcare providers to follow before proceedings can even be commenced. Failure to follow the protocol may have **adverse costs implications** if proceedings are nonetheless commenced. Under this Protocol the claimant must set out the basis of his claim against the healthcare provider and the amount of money (or at least the broad areas of damages) he wants. The healthcare provider must provide a substantive reply **within three months**. Already this timetable is proving extremely difficult for healthcare providers to meet.

Once proceedings are commenced, the landscape appears a little more familiar: the claimant issues a **claim form** and sets out the essence of the claim (though not the evidence in detail) in **particulars of claim** (in a document technically now called his **statement of case** [1], the new phrase for what used to be called **pleadings**); the defendant sends back a **defence** (again now referred to technically as his statement of case); the parties then provide disclosure [2] of documents, that is to say they indicate which relevant documents they hold.

But then the procedure once again veers off into hitherto unknown realms. Cases are **allocated** [3] to one of three **tracks**, the **small claims track, fast track** and **multi-track**, depending on their value and complexity. Most clinical negligence actions will be allocated to the multi-track, which provides the most flexibility. The Court now plays an active part in **managing** the action, to ensure that timetables are adhered to and to monitor the conduct of the parties. Thus most lawyers now have some experience of attending a **case management conference**, when the court will make directions for the management of the case until trial.

Many lawyers (and some doctors) were very worried before the new rules came into effect that the courts would attempt to impose **single joint experts** in clinical negligence cases. However, although there is provision for a single joint expert to be used, these will be very rare in practice in clinical negligence actions, especially on issues of breach of duty and causation. There is growing use of single joint experts on certain issues of quantum (e.g. future physiotherapy needs for brain damaged babies). What will become more and more common (indeed it is already expected in most if not all cases) is that the relevant experts will meet before trial to try and narrow the issues [4]. (Some have pointed out that this raises a fundamental issue about open justice in the context of Article 6 of the European Convention on Human Rights. To date the civil courts have not been interested in such arguments.)

A defendant who, recognising some vulnerability in his case, wishes to **protect his position** on costs may make a **payment into court** of a sum of money which he believes reasonably reflects the value of the claim. A claimant who wins less money at the eventual trial than the amount the defendant has paid into court will be responsible for all the **defendant's costs** from the date the payment into court was made. It is this provision which has achieved some notoriety in the media following cases in which the claimant has lost most of the award of damages by having to pay a vast proportion of the defendant's costs having failed to beat the payment into court. A payment into court (like a negotiated settlement) does not mean that breach of duty or causation are formally admitted. It should also be added that, if the defendant wins completely, any money paid into court is simply returned to him. Under the **CPR**, a claimant can now make an **offer to settle** to the defendant for a certain sum of money. If he wins more in damages at trial than his offer, the defendant will be penalised by having to pay **punitive interest** on those damages from the date of the offer to settle. The combined effect of the provisions as to payments into court and offers to settle is to narrow down the scope of the trial and make the parties aware of how wide their differences are [5].

Trials (what few there are nowadays) in fact look very similar under the CPR to before. We will probably see in future much more written argument before the trial itself, but the examination of witnesses in open court will still play a fundamental role in the resolution of clinical negligence actions. A judge will still give **judgment** (note the spelling, and note that he or she will not call it an "opinion" or "verdict") having heard oral evidence and oral legal argument as before.

It is said that the law needed fifty years to resolve the procedural changes brought about by the Judicature Acts of the 1870s, no doubt keeping some (perhaps most) lawyers in business far beyond their sell-by date in the process. The recent procedural changes are no less significant. To date, however, they appear to be resulting in increased co-operation between the lawyers for each party and more out of court settlements. It will of course be many years before one can accurately assess the full impact.

References

1. CPR Part 16.
2. CPR Part 31.
3. CPR Parts 26-30.
4. See generally CPR Part 35.
5. See generally CPR Part 36.

Further Reading*

1. The Civil Court Practice: 2000. Butterworths Law 2000.
2. Civil Court Service Jordans 2000.
3. Loughlin P. Civil procedure. Cavendish Publishing 2000.
4. Ingman T. The English legal process, 8th Ed. Blackstone Press 2000.
5. The White Book Service 2000: Civil Procedure. Sweet and Maxwell 2000.

PART II - Further Reading*

1. Harcup J, Waring M, Lanoe M. Advanced litigation: personal injury and clinical negligence, 7th Ed. Jordan 2000.
2. Khan M, Robson M. Clinical Negligence, 2nd Ed. Cavendish Publishing Ltd. 2000.
3. Freeman M, Lewis A, Eds. Law and Medicine. Oxford University Press 2000.
4. Leung. Law for Doctors. Blackwell Science Ltd. 2000.
5. Healy J. Medical Negligence: common law experiences. Sweet and Maxwell 1999.
6. Jones M. Medical Negligence, 3rd Ed. Sweet and Maxwell 2001.
7. McLean SAM, Ed. Law reform and medical injury litigation. Dartmouth 1995.
8. Action for Victims of Medical Accidents, Thomas L, Vincent C, MacNeil P, Eds. Medical accidents and the law: a practical guide for patients and their advisors. Chancery Wiley Law Publications 1998.
9. Teff H, Ed. Medical practice and malpractice. Dartmouth 2001.
10. Harper RS. Medical treatment and the law: the protection of adults and minors in the family division. Jordans 1999.

11. Francis R, Johnston C. Medical treatment decisions and the law. Butterworths Law 2000.

12. O'Grady J, Dodds-Smith I, Spencer M, Eds. Medicines, medical devices and the law. Greenwich Medical Media 1999.

13. Nelson-Jones R, Burton F. Nelson-Jones & Burton: medical negligence case law, 2nd Ed. Butterworths Law 1995.

14. Kennedy & Grubb. Principles of medical law. Oxford University Press 1999.

15. Powers M, Harris N, Lockhart-Mirams A, Eds. Clinical Negligence, 3rd Ed. Butterworths Law 2000.

16. Branthwaite M. Law for doctors: principles and practicalities. Royal Society of Medicine Press Ltd. 2000.

17. Kennedy & Grubb. Medical Law - Text and Materials, 2nd Edition Butterworths 1994.

* All books appearing in this list do not necessarily reflect an endorsement by the named authors or the publisher.

PART III

Avoiding
Medico-legal Problems

Chapter 9

Risk management

Risk management is a fundamental modern concept in reducing the chance of problems which might lead to litigation. Doctors rightly feel that they make experienced judgements about risk every day, and that many **adverse events** occur by mischance despite good, thoughtful care. But "risk management" involves two important concepts which transcend the everyday handling of risks by **clinicians**.

1. While many problems undoubtedly arise because of individual mischance, a substantial number occur as a direct or indirect result of [1]:

❖   lack of clear policies;

❖   deficient working practices;

❖   poorly defined responsibilities;

❖   inadequate communication;

❖   staff working beyond their competence.

Avoidable problems may occur either as a result of one of these factors, or due to an unforeseen combination of two or more - so called "systems failures".

2. Risk management in a healthcare system like the NHS relates to a whole range of activities and areas, of which direct patient care is simply the best recognised. These include risks relating to buildings and equipment, security, fire, hazardous substances and waste materials. The people who may be harmed and then seek recompense include patients, visitors and staff. All clinicians need to understand that risk management extends well beyond the field of clinical practice, but there should be no question of doctors relegating this concept to the mental backwater usually reserved for fire lectures and the more tedious aspects of "health and safety".

The basic principles involved in risk management have been set out in "Risk Management in the NHS" published in 1994 [1]. They include identifying potential risks; analysing their likelihood, effects, and cost; considering how they might be controlled or eliminated; and deciding how best to insure against risks which cannot be eliminated. These principles can be applied across the whole range of clinical activities.

Clinical risk management: lessons from the United States

The concept and practice of clinical risk management was developed in the United States as a response to the explosion of lawsuits in the 1960s and 1970s. The three main aims were [2]:

❖ to improve claims management - controlling costs by knowing how to gather evidence, when to resist, and when to settle;

❖ to minimise the damage suffered by patients - by recognising problems as early as possible, and managing them appropriately;

❖ to prevent the kinds of adverse outcomes likely to lead to litigation.

Mills and von Bolschwing [2] (risk management specialists in California) believe that the United Kingdom has an advantage over the United

States, because clinical risk management has developed more as a safeguard against potential problems ahead, than as a reaction to an uncontrolled situation. In addition, the United Kingdom has been able to draw on the past experience of the USA.

References

1. Department of Health. Risk management in the NHS. 1994.
2. Mills DH, von Bolschwing GE. Does clinical risk management improve the quality of health care? *Clinical Risk* 1995; 1: 171-4.

Further Reading*

1. Vincent C, Ed. Clinical risk management, 2nd Ed. BMJ Books 2000.
2. Wilson J, Tingle J. Clinical risk management. Butterworth-Heinemann 1997.
3. Lilley R. Making sense of risk management: a workbook for primary care. Radcliffe Medical Press 1999.
4. Mohanna K, Chambers R. Risk matters in healthcare: communicating, explaining and managing risk. Radcliffe Medical Press 2000.
5. Henderson. Sharing the challenge: risks in healthcare practice. Blackwell Science 1999.
6. Vincent C, De Mol B, Eds. Safety in medicine. Pergamon 2000.
7. Clements RV. Essentials of clinical risk management. In Ed. Vincent C. London. BMA Publications 1995.

* All books appearing in this list do not necessarily reflect an endorsement by the named authors or the publisher.

Chapter 10

Clinical
incident reporting

Incident reporting by clinicians was pioneered in the United States as part of the response to escalating litigation, and defence organisations in the United Kingdom started to encourage this practice in the 1970s and 1980s. Latterly, the setting up of **clinical incident reporting** systems has become part of the risk management strategy of all NHS hospitals, and is an explicit requirement of the Clinical Negligence Scheme for Trusts (CNST) [1].

Alerting hospital management to any incident which might result in a complaint or medico-legal claim allows a coordinated response to:

❖ treating the adverse event and optimising clinical care of the patient;

❖ communicating thoroughly with the patient and their relatives;

❖ ensuring that documentation is complete;

❖ obtaining statements from relevant staff (if there is a need) while events are still fresh in their minds;

❖ informing legal liaison teams of potentially serious events at an early stage (both to prepare a defence and to anticipate potential liability).

In addition, incident reporting allows adverse events to be recorded on databases at local, regional, or national level: the latter is currently being advocated by government in the United Kingdom [2]. Collating adverse clinical events in this way should allow patterns and recurring themes to be recognised, so that practice can be changed accordingly. In the United States data have been published about the kinds of adverse events which have precipitated law suits [3] and the defence organisations in the United Kingdom regularly publish lists and examples of cases which have resulted in claims [4-7].

What kinds of "incidents" should be reported?

Historically in the United Kingdom incident reporting was associated with safety issues and accident reports [8]. Reporting was (and still is) incumbent upon nurses in a much more strictly defined form than for medical staff. Nursing reports involve incidents such as falls, injuries (ranging from needle-stick to back injuries) and drug administration errors.

Taking a wider perspective, the national confidential reports - initially the **Confidential Report into Maternal Deaths**, and latterly the **National Confidential Enquiry into Perioperative Deaths (NCEPOD)** [9] have represented a form of clinical incident reporting. Their aim has been to identify areas of clinical practice, organisation, and provision of facilities which may have contributed to deaths, and which might therefore be improved. They have no bearing on individual cases (the data are protected by Crown Indemnity and are destroyed) although the publication of recognisable vignettes has caused anxiety among many surgeons.

At a local level reporting of "clinical incidents" by medical staff has been explicitly encouraged in recent years, but the definition of incidents and the mandate to report them remains rather vague. This offers doctors the opportunity to use their judgement, and to report incidents which <u>they</u> think might result in dissatisfaction on the part of patients or relatives (for example following faultless care, but a patient or relatives who are complaining loudly nevertheless). Rather than grasping this opportunity, doctors have in general been reluctant to report clinical incidents. The likely reasons for this are:

❖   uncertainty about how reports will be used by management;

❖   fear that reports will be used to discipline them;

❖   concern that they are somehow admitting negligence or guilt (particularly when they feel that they have done their best);

❖   lack of concern about possible medico-legal liability;

❖   lack of time in an overburdened schedule;

❖   concern that if they are assiduous in reporting, then they (and their hospital) may feature excessively in any database or "league table" of reported incidents.

While these concerns are all understandable, there remains a mandate (specifically from CNST) to report incidents with a view to minimising medico-legal liability [1]. Other than the reasonable aims of this system (listed above) doctors who feel disinclined to participate in incident reporting should perhaps consider the following points:

❖   the whole aim of the system is to offer them the best medico-legal protection;

❖   submitting a report immediately shares responsibility for dealing with the incident - they are no longer alone in trying to resolve the problem;

❖   there should be no need to complete laborious forms - they ought to be able to dictate a report just like any other letter or operation note;

❖   if they do not complete an incident report, somebody else (for example a nurse who has been involved) may quite reasonably and properly do so - this is likely to be less acceptable to the responsible doctor, both in principle and in content;

❖ if they have not submitted a clinical incident report for an event which has clearly been the result of sub-standard practice, and which becomes the subject of a medico-legal claim then they could very reasonably be censured.

Sadly, there will never be a solution to the dilemma that departments or hospitals which record and report problems thoroughly will appear superficially to have larger numbers of adverse events than those which do not. This applies equally to incident reports for medico-legal purposes and complications recorded as part of clinical audit. In the final analysis, however, a transparently thorough and assiduous reporting system is likely to reflect well on any hospital, and should ensure that it emerges with credit from any detailed examination (for example by CNST).

References

1. Clinical Negligence Scheme for Trusts. Risk management standards. London. National Health Service Litigation Authority. 2000.
2. Department of Health. An organisation with a memory. Report of on expert group on learning from adverse events chaired by the Chief Medical Officer. Norwich. The Stationery Office. 2000.
3. Mills DH, von Bolschwing GE. Does clinical risk management improve the quality of health care? *Clinical Risk* 1995; 1: 171-4.
4. *The Journal of the Medical Defence Union.* Published by the Medical Defence Union, 3 Devonshire Place, London W1N 2EA.
5. *Casebook.* The Journal for the Members of the Medical Protection Society. Published by the Medical Protection Society, Granary Wharf House, Leeds, LS11 5PY.
6. *Summons.* The Medical & Dental Defence Union of Scotland, Mackintosh House, 120 Blythswood Street, Glasgow, G2 4EA.
7. *Notes.* St Paul International Insurance Company Limited, 61-63 London Road, Redhill, Surrey RH1 1NA.
8. Lindgren O, Haywood B. Clinical incident reporting in NHS Trusts. *Health Care Risk Report* 1996 (May); 15-7.
9. The National Confidential Enquiry into Perioperative Deaths (NCEPOD). The Royal College of Surgeons of England, 35-43 Lincoln's Inn Fields, London WC2A 3PN.

Chapter 11

Guidelines

and

the law

Surgeons are concerned about the proliferation of clinical guidelines, and the medico-legal risks they face if they practice outside their recommendations. Other concerns about guidelines are [1]:

❖ their quality varies: some have a good scientific **evidence base** while others do not;

❖ different clinical guidelines about the same subject may contain conflicting advice;

❖ many guidelines consider only clinical consequences, and not cost issues (this may make them impossible to implement);

❖ guidelines are often not readily accessible at the time they are needed;

❖ they may be too complicated to follow easily.

There is a fear in the minds of many clinicians that while guidelines may allow some freedom of decision in the eyes of the law, clinical **protocols** may not, and that failure to adhere to a protocol will automatically leave them open to an accusation of negligence in the context of a medico-legal claim. This section will provide reassurance that reasonable and properly planned departure from guidelines ought to be acceptable from a legal point of view: it is entirely reasonable to apply all the same arguments to clinical protocols.

In addition to clinical guidelines, there are also Health Service guidelines which are produced primarily for managers of the service. This section will concentrate on clinical guidelines, which are aimed at doctors and others involved directly in patient care.

The purpose of guidelines

Guidelines can be defined as [2] "systematically designed statements to assist practitioner and patient decisions about appropriate health care for specific clinical circumstances". Guidelines are often created with an aim of trying to reduce variations in practice (especially when some practices are demonstrably less good than others). They may also aim to improve efficiency and to reduce costs [3].

Departing from guidelines in patient management

Guidelines are no more mandatory than the word implies and the definition (above) suggests: they are a "guide", and they are designed to "assist" clinicians. Whether a surgeon decides to apply a particular guideline to an individual patient is entirely a matter of clinical judgement. Guidelines may contain some statements which have a sound evidence base and describe universal practice; some which are based on the little evidence but common practice; and others which are based on no good evidence at all in areas for which there is wide variation in clinical practice. The medico-legal position of a surgeon who failed to apply a particular guideline statement in the management of a patient would be very different for the first of these compared with the last. In either case the <u>Bolam</u> principle and the judgement of the court would apply - did the surgeon act reasonably?

The most important aspect of departing from guidelines in patient management is being able to justify the reason, and this is far better done by making a record at the time, rather than providing a reason in retrospect. There should never be a serious medico-legal problem for the surgeon who departs from guidelines in treating a patient, and who documents a reasonable explanation at the time. This is good clinical practice.

The situation is different if a surgeon pursues management which departs from the recommendations of established guidelines because of ignorance (either ignorance that the guidelines existed or ignorance of their content). This does pose a medico-legal threat, and if the surgeon admits that he would have managed the patient differently if he had known the guidelines, then he may be judged negligent (see Hucks v Cole [1993] 4 Med LR 393).

Another possible scenario involves a claim against a clinician who has applied guidelines inappropriately and has harmed a patient by doing so. That doctor might well be found negligent [4].

Guidelines as evidence

Guidelines may be used by experts in medico-legal proceedings to support their opinions about accepted and common practice, but they are not in themselves a substitute for an expert opinion. From a legal standpoint guidelines are effectively hearsay [5].

The date of publication of guidelines

This is an important consideration. If the relevant guidelines had not been published at the time the patient was treated then there can be no expectation for the surgeon to have followed them. The courts also appreciate that doctors need a certain length of time to assimilate guidelines after their publication: this interval will vary depending on the circumstances, and may in future be influenced by the theoretically immediate availability of guidelines on the internet. Conversely, guidelines can become outdated and inappropriate with advances in management.

It is important that all guidelines (including local ones) are dated, and that revisions are also dated. A copy of each revision should always be retained for medico-legal purposes. Ideally they should be published with an intended revision date.

Guidelines from different sources

Guidelines originate from a plethora of sources, including:

❖ individual departments or groups of clinicians dealing with a particular clinical problem;

❖ clinicians within a single hospital, Trust, or Health Authority;

❖ national professional societies, Royal Colleges, or other national groups;

❖ the **National Institute for Clinical Excellence (NICE)**.

Guidelines developed locally by groups of clinicians working together have the advantage of local "ownership" [6], while those produced by influential national bodies inevitably have the cachet of being authoritative. Many clinicians perceive potential difficulties in determining which of these guidelines are more "important" than others when more than one exists in a particular area. In practice this kind of concern should be needless, because if there is really good evidence about a point of management then the guidelines ought to concur. Discordance is most likely over points for which evidence is not compelling and for which practice varies: the usual question of whether or not a doctor's actions were reasonable will apply - various guidelines notwithstanding.

Legal action against the authors of guidelines

If a patient suffers harm, and the responsible doctors use adherence to guidelines as part of their defence, then is there a risk that the authors of those guidelines might in turn be sued? Newdick [3] has considered this question and concluded that this is unlikely, because the doctors involved in treating a patient should be responsible for deciding whether a guideline was appropriate or not. In addition, the authors of guidelines owe no duty of care to the patient.

References

1. National Institute for Clinical Excellence. A guide to our work. London. NHS National Institute for Clinical Excellence. 1999.
2. NHS Centre for Reviews and Dissemination. Implementing clinical practice guidelines. London. FT Healthcare. 1994.
3. Newdick C. The status of guidelines. *Health Care Risk Report* 1996 (October); 14-5.
4. Hurwitz B. Legal and political considerations of clinical practice guidelines. *BMJ* 1999; 318: 661-4.
5. Collins J. Guidelines in clinical practice. *Journal of the Medical Defence Union* 1998; 14: 4.
6. Muir Gray JA. Evidence-based, locally owned, patient-centred guideline development. *Br J Surg* 1997; 84: 1636-7.

Further Reading*

1. Eccles M, Grimshaw J, Eds. Clinical guidelines: from conception to use. Radcliffe Medical Press 2000.
2. Hurwitz B. Clinical guidelines and the law. Radcliffe Medical Press 1999.

---

*   All books appearing in this list do not necessarily reflect an endorsement by the named authors or the publisher.

Chapter 12

Consent

Problems relating to consent underpin the bulk of medico-legal claims in surgery [1-3]. Most could be avoided or ameliorated by thorough, effective communication between surgeon and patient, and more explicit record keeping.

Legal requirements for consent

Some kind of consent is necessary before any physical contact with a patient - even physical examination, otherwise an accusation of *assault* is possible. Consent may simply be *implied* (for example by the patient attending a clinic, undressing, and lying down on the couch) or it may be *express* consent - in other words specific oral or written consent for a particular examination or procedure. Whether a patient has consented or not is a question of fact: the existence of a signed consent form may help to determine the answer, but is not necessarily conclusive. Three conditions need to be fulfilled for consent to be legally valid:

1. *The patient must be capable of giving consent.* For most normal adult patients this does not pose a problem: it becomes an issue when dealing with people who are mentally compromised, and with children.

    The capacity to give consent may depend on the kind of intervention which is proposed. A patient with limited intellectual capacity might be deemed capable of giving consent for a simple procedure, but not for one which has more complex implications.

2. *The patient should be sufficiently informed.* The amount of information given to a patient, and how much they retain, are discussed in specific sections below.

3. *The consent must be given voluntarily.* Consent *obtained by physical or mental duress or fraud is likely to be ruled invalid.* The following is an interesting example:

> *A 35 year old Roman Catholic woman was sterilised during a caesarean section operation. The question of sterilisation had been raised only after she had been in labour for a long time, and when she had been given opiate analgesia. Subsequently she regretted the decision and took the Health Authority to court with a claim which alleged assault. The judge dismissed this claim, but nevertheless awarded the patient £3,000 in damages on the grounds that there had been negligence in failing to counsel her adequately about an operation with such important consequences.*

Informed consent

The phrase **informed consent** should be used with some caution, as it has a specific meaning for lawyers. To an English lawyer, informed consent denotes a US-style patient-centred approach to consent, which uses the concept of the reasonable patient in order to determine the amount of information which must be given. English law adopts at the moment a doctor-centred approach, in that the test for determining how much information must be given is determined by the doctor, to be judged by the standard of the <u>Bolam</u> test. Whether English law will change is discussed below.

How much should patients be told?

These principles have left the decision about how much to tell patients primarily in the hands of doctors, based on consideration of the individual patient and the circumstances of the planned procedure. However, they provide no specific guidance for surgeons about what "threshold" of risks to impart to patients or about different clinical circumstances. The next sections deal with these dilemmas in turn.

What risks should patients be told about when seeking informed consent?

The leading case on consent for medical treatment in English law is Sidaway v Bethlem Royal Hospital [1985] AC 871, HL. The patient suffered persistent pain in her neck and shoulders and was advised by a surgeon to have an operation on her spinal column to relieve the pain. The surgeon warned her of the possibility of disturbing a nerve root and the possible consequences of doing so but did not mention the possibility of damage to the spinal cord, even though he would be operating within 3mm of it. The risk of damage to the spinal cord was very small (less than 1%) but if the risk materialised the injury could range from mild to very severe. The patient duly consented and the operation was carried out with reasonable skill and care. However, the patient suffered an injury to her spinal cord which resulted in her being severely disabled. The patient lost at trial and before the Court of Appeal. The House of Lords held that:

❖ the test for determining liability in respect of a doctor's duty to warn his patient of risks inherent in treatment recommended by him was the Bolam test, i.e. which requires the doctor to act in accordance with a standard accepted as proper by a responsible body of medical opinion;

❖ although a decision on what risks should be disclosed for the particular patient is primarily a matter of clinical judgment, the disclosure of a particular risk of serious adverse consequences might be so obviously necessary for the patient to make a decision about the operation that no reasonably prudent doctor would fail to disclose the risk;

73

❖ when questioned specifically by a patient of apparently sound mind about the risks involved in a particular treatment, the doctor is obliged to answer truthfully and as fully as the questioner requires.

In Sidaway the claimant lost because the trial judge applied the correct test (the Bolam test) to the evidence. The claimant could not show that the doctor had failed to act in accordance with a responsible body of medical opinion.

Lord Scarman was the only Law Lord who took the view that informed consent, that is to say patient-centred information, should become part of English law. To date it has not done so, except perhaps by the back door.

In *The Surgeon's Duty of Care* (subtitled *Guidance for surgeons on ethical and legal issues*) [4] the Senate of Surgery of Great Britain and Ireland sets out what information should be given to a patient before treatment. It was followed by *Seeking Patients' Consent - the ethical considerations* [5], in which the GMC also explain what information should be given to a patient before treatment. This document requires full informed consent by any other name. In future, it will become increasingly difficult for a doctor to say that, in explaining the nature of proposed treatment, he has satisfied the Bolam test if he fails to come up to the standard which the GMC has imposed. The US-style doctrine of informed consent has probably therefore been imposed on the profession by its own regulatory body.

In practice, claims based solely on lack of information (and therefore no true consent) before treatment invariably fail because the patient cannot persuade a court that he would not have undergone the treatment if he had been told about the relevant risk. The doctor will always be able to argue (and will usually succeed in arguing) that the patient would have undergone the treatment in any event, so the claim will fail on causation.

If there is a risk of a very serious complication (for example paraplegia) then the patient should be informed, even if the risk is small (for example one in thousands). This kind of risk is conveniently presented as part of the written information given to the patient, unless a surgeon considers that knowledge of it may influence the patient's decision to proceed, or unless the patient specifically asks to be told about "all the risks". This suggestion does not imply that information should be withheld in any way: this is only permissible if a doctor judges that disclosure of particular information would cause the patient serious harm.

The surgeon is obliged to answer, honestly as possible, any questions the patient asks about risks and benefits, in as much detail as the patient requires. This may include information about the risks of a procedure in the hands of that particular surgeon or institution, compared with other surgeons or hospitals.

The clinical circumstances

English law allows clinicians considerable and sensible latitude to decide on what degree of informed consent is necessary depending on the clinical circumstances. The judgement on the Sidaway case means that the duty to warn a patient about all possible risks is likely to be seen as less for an emergency, life-saving operation on an acutely ill patient (for example a patient with a ruptured **aortic aneurysm**) than for a patient facing an **elective** and non-essential procedure (for example varicose vein surgery). Indeed, when consent cannot be obtained in an emergency it is legitimate for a doctor to provide whatever treatment is immediately necessary to save life or avoid significant deterioration in health [5].

Using the example of leaking aortic aneurysm, it seems reasonable to assume that the shocked patient would be able to make as much of a "rational decision" as is possible by being told simply that they need a major operation to save their life. Thrusting more information about risks would seem irrelevant, unkind and a waste of precious time. If the patient is unconscious then no counselling is possible and it is unlikely that any subsequent medico-legal proceedings would succeed if a surgeon operated in the belief that surgery was in the best interests of the patient, yet without express consent.

Although advice to the patient may be minimal in emergency circumstances, it seems sensible to advise close relatives as explicitly and sympathetically as possible. After all, it is they who might sue if the patient dies, and they are likely to exert a strong influence on any decision to take legal action if major complications occur. Explaining the situation and prognosis to them in a kind way therefore offers the surgeon considerable medico-legal protection - quite apart from being an important element of good medical practice.

As an extension of any pre-operative counselling of relatives, I advocate talking to the next of kin (usually by telephone) immediately after any emergency operation. This is always greatly appreciated, and enhances the relationship with the patient's family. It is a good time to prepare them for an adverse outcome if all has not gone well. It indicates a degree of concern and openness which makes inappropriate complaints or subsequent legal claims unlikely.

Counselling before elective procedures needs nowadays to be very thorough, especially if the operation is not essential. In general and vascular surgery, for example, the commonest operation followed by successful claims is varicose vein surgery [2]. In urology vasectomy is a specific example; and any purely aesthetic procedure demands particularly explicit pre-operative advice. The patient's expectations, and their knowledge of possible problems should be on a par with those of the surgeon.

Cases which are neither dire emergencies, nor truly elective, can present special problems. How fully should the patient with an urgent problem mandating operation be confronted with all the possible risks, when clinical judgement and common sense dictate that these will not influence their decision to proceed? Examples might be the patient with bowel obstruction or with an acutely **ischaemic** leg. In the first case counselling about a possible **stoma** would seem essential, and in the second the possibility of limb loss must be explained, since these are the main specific concerns. Many surgeons would consider it unkind to burden the patient with the knowledge of all other possible complications when this would almost certainly not change the patient's mind about consent, but would add still more (probably needless) worries to a situation which is already distressing to them. This applies particularly to the elderly, frightened patient. Giving them an "American style" consent form which sets out all possible risks is one solution, but it is in a sense a "fudge" because the patient may choose not to read it. Giving a specific advice booklet (see below) is another alternative which gives them the opportunity to read about risks if they want (and the giving of the booklet should, of course, be recorded in their notes).

This kind of situation exemplifies the dilemma between acting as a "good doctor" by being sensitive to the emotional welfare of the patient (protecting them from distressing knowledge which is unlikely to influence decisions) and taking steps to protect against the very small risk of subsequent accusations of failure to inform.

Consent for children and mentally impaired adults

Whether a patient is competent to give consent is a question of fact and degree in every individual case. The law presumes (but no more) that adults and children over 16 are competent to consent. The patients usually dealt with in legal judgments about "tailoring information to the patient" are, therefore, usually minors, and those who have some kind of obvious mental impairment.

Minors (children)
In general, parents or guardians need to be counselled and to give express consent to treatment for children under the age of sixteen. The law is clear that parental consent is not required when a minor aged sixteen to eighteen has consented to treatment.

The case commonly cited regarding consent and children under the age of sixteen is that of Gillick v West Norfolk and Wisbech Area Health Authority [1985] 3 WLR 830, HL. Following the publication in 1981 of a Department of Health and Social Security memorandum stating that contraceptive advice or treatment might, in exceptional circumstances, be given to people under sixteen without the consent of their parents,

CHAPTER 12

Mrs Victoria Gillick wrote to the West Norfolk and Wisbech Area Health Authority demanding an assurance that her daughters would not be prescribed contraceptives while they were under sixteen years old. When the Health Authority refused to provide such an assurance she took legal action against them, and appealed to the House of Lords when judgment was given against her. In his speech Lord Fraser of Tullybelton stated that:

"provided the patient whether a boy or girl is capable of understanding what is proposed, and of expressing his or her own wishes, I see no good reason for holding that he or she lacks the capacity to express them validly and effectively and to authorise the medical man to make the examination or give the treatment which he advises".

A similar legal ruling exists in Scotland, based on the capacity of a child to understand the proposed treatment. The Age of Legal Capacity (Scotland) Act 1991 states that a person under sixteen can give valid consent provided that:

"in the opinion of a qualified medical practitioner attending him, he is capable of understanding the nature and possible consequences of the procedure or treatment".

In surgical practice the issue of consent for children will seldom present problems. It is important to talk directly to all children anyway, adapting what is said to their age and understanding, and then to turn to their parents to cover issues which may concern them more - including possible adverse effects of treatment. Particular sensitivity is needed with some teenagers, who may find examination or discussions embarrassing in front of their parents, but in general a situation can almost always be achieved in which both child and parents are of one mind. Parents can then sign the consent form for an acquiescent patient who is under sixteen years of age. Again, as a matter of personal practice, I would always suggest that a patient of sixteen years or older should sign their own consent form, involving their parents as much as they wish.

The children of Jehovah's Witnesses and blood transfusion

The religious objection of Jehovah's Witnesses to blood transfusion is a particular issue which causes surgeons concern when dealing with these patients. A specific problem arises when there is a clinical need to give blood to a child of a Jehovah's Witness. Under these circumstances, the doctor should seek the Court's permission to give a blood transfusion. The Court will always grant such permission. In addition, the parents will understand that their view has been overridden by a competent authority. It is helpful when dealing with these patients to have read the Code of Practice for the Surgical Management of Jehovah's Witnesses (Royal College of Surgeons of England) [6], and to seek legal advice.

Mentally impaired adults

The Mental Health Act 1983 deals explicitly with the problem of treatment for mental disorders, but not with consent for treatment of physical problems. For a mentally impaired child, parental consent is appropriate and necessary, but nobody else has the right to give consent for an adult with mental incapacity. The way in which such patients might be dealt with was clarified by the decision of the House of Lords in the case of F v West Berkshire Health Authority [1990] 2 AC 1, HL:

> F was a woman of 36 with severe mental incapacity, who lived permanently in a mental hospital. She started a sexual relationship with another patient, and her carers thought that sterilisation would be in her best interests. F was not capable of understanding the implications of the situation or giving consent, and the decision about the lawfulness of the operation was referred to the courts.

In deciding that sterilisation would be in the best interests of F, the Law Lords stated that:

❖ doctors caring for any such patient are obliged to act in accordance with a responsible body of medical opinion, in whatever manner protects the best interests of that patient;

79

❖ doctors should not simply be <u>able</u> to treat the patient with regard to their best interests and without express consent, but should be <u>obliged</u> to do so;

❖ involving other interested parties, such as the patient's relatives and carers in any decisions is good practice;

❖ in the specific case of sterilisation, it is desirable to involve the courts in the decision, but for most kinds of treatment the responsible doctors should make decisions based on the best interests of the patient.

Patients whose capacity to give consent is in doubt

This is, in some ways, a more difficult group than either children or patients who have clear mental incapacity. The assumption must be that every adult has the capacity to consent to treatment, or to refuse:

> *Re C (Adult : Refusal of medical treatment) [1994] 1 All*
> *ER 819. A patient will be competent if he or she can:*
> *comprehend information, it having been presented to*
> *them in a clear way; believe it; and retain it long enough*
> *to weigh it up and make a decision.*

If a patient makes a decision which seems irrational or which is not in tune with the doctor's opinion of what is in their best interests, then the first step should be to "review their information needs" [5]: their apparently irrational decision cannot be held as evidence that they are incompetent. When presented with all the relevant information, and after discussion of all the pros and cons, a competent adult may still choose to make a decision which appears irrational, and it is their right to do so. The BMA/Law Society publication "Assessment of Mental Capacity: Guidance for Doctors and Lawyers" [7] provides further guidance.

Another difficult situation involves *patients whose mental capacity fluctuates*, so that they seem competent to give informed consent at one time, and not at another. This is particularly common in the elderly. The two important steps to take from a medico-legal standpoint are:

❖ record details of the discussion held at the time they seemed competent and gave consent;

❖ review the decision with them at intervals before the start of treatment, and keep a record of these reviews.

Advance directives or "living wills"

These are becoming increasingly common, and assume importance when a patient presents at a time when they are unable to give informed consent (either because of deterioration of an existing condition, or as an emergency). Advance directives must be respected, unless there is good evidence that the patient may have changed their mind. Quite apart from formal advance directives, any known wishes of a patient should be taken into account - these are most usually proffered by relatives or carers.

Ways of giving information to patients

The information which should be available to patients when seeking informed consent is set out in detail in the GMC booklet "Seeking patients' consent: the ethical considerations" [5] (see Appendix I). This includes the nature and prognosis of their condition; the prognosis without treatment; alternative treatment options and their likely outcome. It is reasonable for patients to expect details of the recovery; the likely period of incapacity; the amount of pain and discomfort; and other probable sequelae of the intervention (for example bruising after varicose vein surgery; disturbed bowel habit after bowel resection; bleeding after injection of haemorrhoids). Imparting all this information in the time available for many NHS outpatient consultations is difficult, and most patients are unable to retain more than a fraction of what they have been told. It is therefore important to consider the ways in which information can be given, and by which it can be recorded so that an effort has been made to inform the patient fully.

81

By word of mouth

Despite the fact that patients are only likely to retain a proportion of the details, the consultation remains the primary way in which important information is conveyed, and the setting in which decisions about treatment are made. It is only by face to face discussion that the patient has the chance to ask questions, with a view to shared decision making. This should be the prelude to all clinical interventions and, if done well, should avoid a lot of the litigation which results from inappropriate patient expectations. Keeping an adequate written record of the consultation is important, as discussed above.

By letter

Use of this medium is surprisingly infrequent. Letters represent a clear record of the giving of information, and can be used in two main ways.

❖ Sending the patient a copy of the letter to the referring doctor, containing details of what the patient was told, the choices offered, and relevant specific comments about risks, benefits, or matters particular to that individual patient. Obviously there will be parts of any medical letter which patients are unlikely to understand - I tell them "Some of the letter will be in technical language, but the choices will be clear". Sending copy letters to selected patients in this way involves no extra effort for the surgeon; it informs the patient and makes them feel fully involved in the process of decision making; it allows them time to reflect; and it provides good evidence of what they were told.

❖ Sending a letter to the patient after receiving the results of investigations, telling them about the results and putting in writing advice about proposed treatments, including pros and cons, and specific individual considerations which might affect their choice. This has the advantages of usually avoiding another outpatient appointment; giving the patient time to consider their decision and discuss matters with their family (emphasize this in the letter if it seems especially relevant); and providing precise documented evidence of what they were told. Asking the patient to respond to a letter provides further evidence of their involvement in the decision and their wish to proceed.

Patient information booklets

While the primary purpose of written information is to help the patient, it should also have an important risk management aim, providing explicit evidence that the patient was informed of risks. All patient information material should be designed with this in mind, but with an eye to a sensible balance between risk management information and information about the condition being treated, what happens during treatment, and the recovery. It may be helpful to consider the following suggestions, aimed at maximising the risk management and medico-legal value of information booklets:

❖ there should be a local process for checking the risk management content of patient information material approved and used by the hospital;

❖ an introductory section or paragraph asking patients to read about risks may be an advantage, because it provides one extra piece of evidence of an attempt to inform patients about risks. An example (written by the author and used in Exeter) is:

> *We expect you to make a rapid recovery after your operation and to experience no serious problems. However, it is important that you should know about minor problems which are common after the operation, and also about more serious problems which can just occasionally occur. The section "What problems can occur after the operation?" describes these, and we would particularly ask you to read this.*

❖ the fact that a booklet has been given to a patient should always be recorded in the health record;

❖ booklets should be reviewed and updated by the specialists who use them (for example two yearly, and certainly every five years);

❖ booklets should be dated, and copies retained of each updated version, which can then be produced if a patient makes a claim at some time after treatment. The precise content and wording of the booklet they were given needs to be available as evidence.

Simply giving an information booklet and recording this is no substitute for clear counselling about proposed treatment, and making a record of this conversation. It simply offers an additional way of informing the patient, and making an explicit record of the information which they were given and encouraged to read.

Other ways of providing information
These may include videos, tape recordings, or information provided by computer. Whatever form they take, a record needs to be made about what a patient was given or told (although the patient may take a video and never watch it).

Information from other members of the team
While the surgeon is the primary person who needs to make a decision about treatment with the patient, other members of the team may be very important in giving them advice, which should also be recorded. These include specialist nurses (for example in breast care, oncology or stoma therapy) and other professions allied to medicine ("PAMs") such as occupational therapists, physiotherapists and speech therapists. "Surgical" patients may also be treated by other disciplines, such as oncologists and **interventional radiologists**, who need to provide specialist advice, and to make a record of this: they will often be instrumental in obtaining informed consent for their own specialist interventions.

Consent Forms

Although the signing of a consent form is often seen as the main evidence of "consent" it is vital to understand that a signed consent form is not proof that a patient has either consented to a specific procedure, nor is it proof that the patient was properly informed. It is simply one piece of evidence (albeit an important one) of the consent process - a process which ought to be properly documented at each stage.

One of the main practical concerns about consent forms is which member of the medical team signs them. The requirements are for "consent to be obtained" by a person who is suitably trained and qualified, and who has sufficient knowledge of the proposed intervention to discuss the risks involved. Commonly, the discussion and decision to operate take place with a senior member of the surgical team, but the signing of the consent form is left to a junior member of the team - understandably, because of the timing of events and the perceived priorities of overburdened senior clinicians. Consultants do not want to waste their time standing over patients while they sign consent forms, and rightly so. In addressing this dilemma, the following practical points are worth considering, because they are the subject of widespread misconception:

❖ there is no legal requirement for the person who has advised the patient and signed the consent form to hand it to them personally;

❖ there is no requirement for anyone to witness the signing of the consent form;

❖ it is actually undesirable to stand over the patient waiting for them to sign: it is preferable to give them time to consider the form without any pressure of time;

❖ the consent form can be signed before admission for their procedure (but if this is done a long time ahead - for example in clinic several months in advance - then a record should be made that they were advised again, and that they confirmed their wish to proceed on admission: indeed, a second consent form can be dealt with by a more junior member of the team at this stage as confirmation).

These considerations mean that systems can be devised locally for signing of consent forms by senior clinicians without the logistic difficulties often encountered around the time of hospital admission.

Medico-legal aspects of the consent form which are clear include:

❖ the identity of the patient and of the clinician signing the form should each be clearly documented;

❖ the form must be dated;

❖ the form must be retained safely in the case notes.

What is less clear is the style in which the intervention should be written on the consent form. This is commonly done in a way which any patient could reasonably claim not to have understood (for example abbreviations like TURBT or EUA; technical descriptions like bilateral saphenopopliteal ligation; or eponyms like Adair's operation or Zadek's procedure). The intervention should ideally be written in words which are understandable to the patient, but this invites a lot of potential debate (some procedures are difficult to describe succinctly other than in technical terms).

It is probably unacceptable to use abbreviations which are incomprehensible to anyone except a specialist, and it is certainly worth considering how best to describe procedures on consent forms in an understandable way [8]. It is always acceptable to write additional information on consent forms before they are signed - for example a record of specific complications about which the patient has been told. The patient may also reasonably ask to add any limitations they want to place on the extent of intervention to which they wish to consent.

Simply as a personal view, it is unfortunate that British law requires the title "Consent form". A form entitled "Request for treatment" (now used in some countries) would be more in tune with the modern concepts of shared decision making and "patient responsibility".

Recording informed consent

The medical notes contain the only tangible evidence of what the patient was told, and keeping a concise but explicit record is therefore vital. A signed consent form provides no evidence that the patient was informed of any particular risks or consequences (unless these are written on the form). If a patient later claims that they were not told (or did not understand) a particular risk or consequence, then this is difficult to refute without good written records. Making records like this is easier for surgeons who do small numbers of major (often high risk) operations and more difficult for those who do large numbers of relatively minor procedures. The latter can pose a particular problem when counselling is necessarily delegated to constantly changing trainees. Measures which can be helpful in defending claims alleging lack of information have been referred to in the various sections above.

❖ Always include a reference to what the patient was told - both in dictated letters and handwritten notes. This may be as brief as "Fully explained to patient" at the end of an entry in the notes. In a clinic letter about the decision to operate the bare minimum should be "I have discussed the risks" but when there are major or specific risks then it is best to record these explicitly. For example, my usual letter about a patient who needs a graft for aortic aneurysm would include:

> *I have discussed the risks of operation and the recovery with Mr. X. In particular, I have told him of the small risk of death (about 4% in my hands); of sexual dysfunction (about 20%); and the tiny risk to each lower limb (less than 1%).*

❖ Record who else was present (" I have advised Mr. X and his wife as follows..."). In cases where there is real medico-legal concern it is helpful to have another member of staff present, and to record this (e.g. "Dr. Strange and Staff Nurse Potts present").

❖ Give the patient written information whenever possible, and record that this has been done.

❖ Make a (tactful) record if the patient seems to have had difficulty grasping what they have been told, or if there seems to have been any other unusual difficulty in imparting information to them.

❖ If there is obvious difficulty in informing the patient because they are ill or mentally impaired, then involve those likely to be concerned with their welfare, such as next of kin, carers, and general practitioners: record who has been consulted.

87

References

1.   Palmer R. Medical negligence - causes, trends and lessons. *Health Care Risk Report* 1998 (October); 1-2.
2.   Goodwin H. Litigation and surgical practice in the UK. *Br J Surg* 2000; 87: 977-9.
3.   Fischer JE. The effect of litigation on surgical practice in the USA. *Br J Surg* 2000; 87: 833-4.
4.   The surgeon's duty of care. The Senate of Surgery of Great Britain and Ireland, 35-43 Lincoln's Inn Fields, London WC2A 3PN. 1997.
5.   Seeking patients' consent: the ethical considerations. General Medical Council. London W1N 6JE. 1998. (See Appendix I).
6.   Code of Practice for the Surgical Management of Jehovah's Witnesses. Royal College of Surgeons of England, 35-43 Lincoln's Inn Fields, London WC2A 3PN. 1996.
7.   Assessment of Mental Capacity - Guidance for Doctors and Lawyers. BMA Professional Division Publications. 1995.
8.   Gladstone J, Campbell B. A model for auditing informed consent. *Journal of Clinical Excellence* 2000; 1: 247-50.

Further Reading*

1.   Hockton A. The law of consent to medical treatment. Sweet and Maxwell. Not yet published.
2.   Mason JK, McCall Smith RA. Law and Medical Ethics, 5th Ed. Butterworths 1999.
3.   Breen K, Cordner S, Plueckhahn V. Ethics, law and medical practice. Allen and Unwin 1997.
4.   Hope et al. Medical Ethics and Law. Churchill Livingstone 2000.
5.   Morgan D. Issues in medical law and ethics. Cavendish Publishing Ltd. 2000.
6.   Baker R, Strosberg MA, Bynum J. Legislating medical ethics: a study of the New York State do-not-resuscitate law. Kluwer Academic Publishers 1995.
7.   McLean S. Old law, new medicine: medical ethics and human rights. Rivers Oram Press 1999.
8.   Harper RS. Medical treatment and the law: the protection of adults and minors in the family division. Jordans 1999.
9.   Francis R, Johnston C. Medical treatment decisions and the law. Butterworths Law 2000.

*   All books appearing in this list do not necessarily reflect an endorsement by the named authors or the publisher.

Chapter 13

Documentation

and

record keeping

Medical records and other hospital documentation are fundamental not only in defending claims, but also in influencing whether dissatisfaction proceeds to a claim in the first instance. When a dissatisfied patient or their relatives request disclosure of the medical records, and seek advice based on them, a meticulous record describing a good standard of care may well sway them and their advisors against proceeding. When a claim is made, then the thoroughness of the records can be a very important factor in the outcome - good record keeping will guarantee the defence of an unreasonable claim, and may lead to successful defence in an arguable one; while poor or absent records are likely to lose the arguable case, and prejudice the defence of one which was otherwise well managed clinically. Poor record keeping is very common [1] and is a major problem in medico-legal actions [2,3]. Some of the reasons for this are:

❖ surgeons in the NHS are under pressure to see large numbers of patients, and have only limited time for each: the writing of records assumes quite low priority when compared with the need to assess the patient and talk to them;

❖ traditionally, thorough note keeping has not been a very important aspect of medical education, and it is not part of the culture of many specialties;

❖ the risk management aspect of record keeping can be very repetitive and boring, especially in specialties with a high throughput of similar patients (for example patients with prostatic symptoms in urology, varicose veins in vascular surgery, breast lumps in breast surgery);

❖ nothing in "the system" forces surgeons to keep thorough records (either in the NHS or privately);

❖ many surgeons see the chance of needing thorough "risk management" records as low, and not worth the time and effort in the context of a pressurised clinical practice.

All these attitudes are understandable, but the reasons they are not sustainable are:

❖ complaints and medico-legal proceedings are becoming so much more frequent, and surgeons will therefore learn from bitter experience;

❖ education of doctors will change to reflect the importance of thorough records;

❖ the gap in record keeping standards between doctors and other health professionals (like nurses) will close with the introduction of integrated patient records and **integrated care pathway**s [4,5];

❖ clinical governance will gradually oblige all clinicians to keep good records.

What records are important?

From a medico-legal standpoint, the term "**health record**" is perhaps better than "**medical record**" or "case notes" because the notes and letters written by doctors are often only a small part of the documentary record (although frequently the most conspicuous, and commonly the least complete). Any documentation about a patient may assume pivotal importance if a claim is made - nursing notes, test results, X rays, drug charts, observation charts, and assessment forms are all potentially vital pieces of evidence of the quality of care. During the rest of this discussion, the phrase "medical record" will be used to refer specifically to the documentation made by doctors.

Retention of health records

The Department of Health has recommended that all health records (including X rays) should be kept for at least eight years after the conclusion of treatment (and that both obstetric notes and children's notes should be retained at least until 25 years after birth) [6-8].

These recommendations have been made because a patient (or their relatives) may start legal proceedings up to three years after the time when they became aware that their medical treatment (or lack of it) may have caused them harm. This may be much longer than three years after the treatment actually took place. "Children" may start action at any time up to the age of 21.

Storage of records (and particularly X rays) poses escalating problems for hospitals and whether any are kept for longer periods than those recommended by the Department of Health is a matter for debate at local level.

The need for contemporaneous medical notes

The details of a major recent case with an adverse outcome are likely to be memorable to any surgeon: but very many medico-legal claims concern minor, "routine" cases, and ones which were dealt with long ago. Without written records, the surgeon may have no detailed recollection of the case. Even more important, a court will be more likely to believe the memory of an aggrieved patient relating to a "life experience" than that of a surgeon for whom the patient was one of many.

91

There is always a tendency to think of "medical notes" as a handwritten screed, but dictated and typed clinical notes, operation notes, and letters all represent good methods for busy surgeons to record their actions, and the thinking behind them. I make extensive use of operation notes and letters (the latter even for inpatient referrals) to record findings, opinions, actions, and the advice given to patients - much of this largely for risk management purposes.

A list of the requirements for adequate medical records potentially makes very dull reading, but the following aims to emphasize some aspects of medical records which can be especially important from a medico-legal standpoint.

❖ All written records should be dated, including the <u>year</u> (which may seem unnecessary at the time, but which may be both vital and uncertain a long time later). Ideally written notes entries should have the time they were written as well as the date: this really is most important for emergency admissions and when dealing with seriously unwell patients, for whom the situation may change rapidly, and several written entries may be made on a single day. Every sheet in the notes should have the patient's name (and unit number within the NHS): it is extraordinary how often this turns out to be missing on parts of the record which are fundamentally important at a later date.

❖ Written records should ideally be contemporaneous - in other words written at or very shortly after the events to which they refer. If they are written later, then this should be made clear (for example - "Patient collapsed 0130. I attended 0140. This note 0415" - avoids later suggestions by relatives that there was a delay, which might be difficult to refute if there were simply a note timed at 0415) [9].

❖ Attempts to alter or add to records are almost invariably detectable, and will have a seriously adverse influence on the defence of a claim.

❖ Notes need to be legible. There is no need for writing to be stylistically beautiful, but other health professionals at least must be able to read it (we use the criterion of legibility by a senior member of the clinical audit staff who was once a nursing sister as the "gold standard" in our local audits of health records [10]).

❖ The writer must be identifiable - by signature, written name, "House Surgeon to Mr. X", bleep number, or some other means likely to allow the person to be sought out some time later.

❖ The style and format of notes must be explicit and objective [3], but in addition it is entirely appropriate to include a record of doubts, concerns, or the reasons for decisions, especially in difficult cases.

❖ If management departs from guidelines or relevant protocols, record this and the reasons for the decision.

❖ Record what patients and their relatives have been told, including the provision of written information. This is dealt with in detail in the section on informed consent. Particularly important matters to put on record are the risks of proposed treatments; information about the diagnosis of cancer; and discussions about palliative care, including decisions not to resuscitate.

❖ Do not write comments about patients which could be construed as rude. This can present a difficult dilemma, as the examples below (both real ones) demonstrate:

Example 1 *The voluminous notes of a patient pursuing a medico-legal claim left the medical expert in some doubt about the character of the patient, because some of the presentations and responses to medical care were most unusual. A brief letter from a consultant, written in 1975, began with the words "This big dim ox...". This single phrase painted a clear picture of the individual. It helped to explain many subsequent events, and might well have been a useful record for other doctors who*

93

saw the patient over the years. Nowadays, however, it would be regarded as improper, and would give grounds for a complaint.

Example 2 *A consultant was asked to see a patient as an inpatient referral (in 1999) whom he found to be very obese, unwilling to mobilise, and unreasonably uncooperative with medical and nursing efforts to aid her. He described the patient in the notes as a "beached elephant seal" and proceeded to draw a picture of a beached elephant seal alongside his comments. This record painted a reasonable picture of the patient and caused amusement among exasperated carers, but it resulted in a complaint which was immediately upheld, and which would have been most prejudicial if medico legal action had ensued for whatever reason.*

It is important to record when patients are uncooperative, or when they seem not to understand what they have been told. However, such records should be couched as objectively as possible, and using words which could be read out in court without creating an impression of rudeness, prejudice, or an attempt to amuse.

❖ Notes should not criticise other practitioners - for example for apparently poor management or delayed referral.

Patients' right of access to health records

The Access to Health Records Act 1990 was largely the result of pressure from clinicians who wanted a greater degree of openness between themselves and their patients [11]. The right of access to health records is now set out in the Data Protection (Subject Access

Modification) (Health) Order 2000, made under the Data Protection Act 1998, which repealed most of the Access to Health Records Act 1990. A data subject (i.e. the patient) may apply to see his health records, and access may only be refused in compelling circumstances. It is this right which makes the phraseology of notes (referred to above) just so important.

Record keeping for medico-legally "high risk" patients

There are certain patients for whom very detailed and explicit recording of events, discussions, and decisions is wise, although defining such cases is difficult. Surgeons ought to be able to recognise circumstances of "high risk" which include:

❖ uncooperative patients, such as those who refuse treatment or discharge themselves from hospital;

❖ patients or relatives who seem ill disposed to their carers, and keen to find fault with their care;

❖ patients with whom discussion and issues around informed consent have been difficult, for whatever reason;

❖ patients whose care has been complicated by adverse events, especially "medical accidents";

❖ patients who are being discharged from hospital, but who may need to return if their symptoms fail to settle (for example the patient with abdominal pain who seems well but who might just possibly have appendicitis). However sympathetically and clearly such patients are advised, they sometimes claim to have been mismanaged if they do need to be readmitted.

It is worth repeating that explicit records are important when departing from usual guidelines or protocols, and when making decisions for palliative care (including "not for resuscitation").

CHAPTER 13

Computerised health records

The strategy of the NHS is now directed towards electronic patient records [1,2]. Computerised documents are, pursuant to the Civil Evidence Act 1995, treated in an entirely equal way to paper records in that they are admissible evidence, by virtue of the definition of 'document' as anything in which information is recorded and copied. It needs to be clear that the record is reliable, which means assurances about security preventing alteration of contemporaneous computerised records.

References

1. The Audit Commission. Setting the records straight. Abingdon. Audit Commission Publications. 1995.
2. Goodwin H. Litigation and surgical practice in the UK. *Br J Surg* 2000; 87: 977-9.
3. Gorney M. Accurate medical records - your primary line of defence. *Health Care Risk Report* 1998 (May): 10-11.
4. Mapping out the patient's journey: experiences of developing pathways of care. Layton A, Moss F, Morgan G. *Quality in Health care.* 1998; 7 (Suppl): S30-S36.
5. de Luc K. Care pathways: an evaluation of their effectiveness. *Journal of Advanced Nursing* 2000; 32: 485-96.
6. Health services management: preservation, retention, and destruction of records: responsibilities of Health Authorities under the Public Records Act. Health Circular (89)20. London. Department of Health. 1989.
7. Preservation, retention, and destruction of maternity (obstetric and midwifery) records. Health Services Guidelines (94)11. London. NHS Management Executive. 1994.
8. For the record: managing records in NHS Trusts and Health Authorities. Health Services Circular 1999/053. Wetherby. Department of Health. 1999.
9. Chapman N. A Coroner's view on the keeping of medical records. *Health Care Risk Report* 1997 (April); 1.
10. Gladstone J, Campbell B. A model for auditing informed consent. *Journal of Clinical Excellence* 2000; 1: 247-50.
11. Jones K. Legal issues of record-keeping. *Health Care Risk Report* 1997 (January); 10-1.
12. NHS Information Authority. Information for health (2. Supporting patient care). http:/www.nhsia.nhs.uk/strategy/full/contents.htm.

Chapter 14

Clinical governance

The term "clinical governance" was introduced in the NHS White Paper of 1998 [1] being derived from the concept of corporate governance in the world of business [2]. The introduction of clinical governance imposed on the chief executives of NHS Trusts responsibility for identifying areas of practice which ought to be improved, and for demonstrating that action had been taken to ensure requisite improvements. This process involves a regular system of reporting to Trust Boards by clinical directorates or other specified groups within each Trust, each led by an individual with personal responsibility for that directorate. A subcommittee responsible for clinical governance now exists in each NHS Trust, chaired by a clinician, and charged with developing the local clinical governance agenda.

There are several elements to clinical governance, but from a medico-legal standpoint the most relevant mandates are for:

❖ good risk reduction programmes;

❖ investigating and learning lessons from adverse events;

❖ putting lessons learnt from complaints into clinical practice;

❖ recognising poor clinical performance and taking action to protect patients from harm.

Governance needs to be underpinned by good information systems and by effective clinical audit. The clinical governance initiative includes a mandate for individual performance review of clinicians, with attention to **continuing professional development (CDP)** and **continuing medical education (CME),** and to job plans.

The clinical governance agenda of every hospital will be influenced by both individual and collated medico-legal claims and complaints; as well as by the reporting of critical and adverse incidents, and accidents. Conversely, the impact of clinical governance on medico-legal work has yet to be seen, but may include:

❖ "flagging up" of problem areas in a particular hospital which might encourage opportunistic medico-legal claims by patients who have received care in that clinical area;

❖ demands from lawyers for information which is known to be available as a result of governance (for example the record of adverse events or complaints relating to a particular surgeon or department);

❖ in the longer term, improvements in systems and practices which will reduce the frequency of medico-legal claims.

References

1. Clinical governance. Quality in the new NHS. HSC 1999/065. Leeds. NHS Executive. 1999.
2. Pincombe C. From clinical risk management to clinical governance. *Health Care Risk Report* 1998; (February); 22-3.

Further Reading*

1. Lugon M, Secker Walker J, Eds. Advancing clinical governance. Royal Society of Medicine Press Ltd. 2000.
2. Chambers R, Boath L. Clinical effectiveness and clinical governance made easy, 2nd Ed. Radcliffe Medical Press 2000.
3. Heard S, Southgate L, Empey D. Clinical governance. Arnold 2000.
4. Scotland A. Clinical governance. Quay Books 1999.
5. Swage T. Clinical governance in healthcare practice. Butterworth Heinemann 2000.
6. Lugon M. Clinical governance: making it happen. Royal Society of Medicine Press Ltd 1999.
7. Dewar S. Clinical governance under construction: problems of design and difficulties in practice. King's Fund 1999.
8. Forman D. Developing clinical governance. Quay Books 1999.
9. Gillies A. Excel for clinical governance. Radcliffe Medical Press 2000.
10. Chambers R, Wakely G. Making clinical governance work for you. Radcliffe Medical Press 2000.
11. Lilley R. Making sense of clinical governance: a workbook for NHS doctors, nurses and managers. Radcliffe Medical Press 1999.
12. Gunn C. A practical guide to complaints handling in the context of clinical governance. Churchill Livingstone 2000.

* All books appearing in this list do not necessarily reflect an endorsement by the named authors or the publisher.

CHAPTER 14 ―――――――――――――――――――――――――――

PART IV

Resolving Complaints
Out of Court

Chapter 15

The

N.H.S. complaints

procedure

In 1991 the Patient's Charter was introduced and since then the Department of Health has encouraged an open attitude to complaints. Patients' expectations have risen and they are more aware of their rights. It is not surprising, therefore, that the number of complaints has increased dramatically. The Community Health Councils (CHCs) were established in 1974 to represent the interests of the public in the National Health Service. These have given help and advice to patients with grievances.

Patient complaints fall into several categories:

❖ they may feel that staff have been rude or indifferent;

❖ they may not have been given sufficient or accurate information;

❖ they may not have received the service or treatment they feel they should;

❖ they may feel that something has gone wrong with their treatment.

Risk management should be organised to try and prevent these causes occurring.

The present NHS complaints procedure (Acting on Complaints [1]) was implemented in 1996. Since then all Trusts and Health Authority Boards have been committed to establish and publicise their written complaints procedure. This complaints procedure is concerned only with resolving complaints and not with disciplinary matters. However, issues considered to be serious may be passed on to the relevant authority or professional regulatory bodies (e.g. General Medical Council). It is recognised that advice and representation may be needed by medical practitioners and this is referred to in Acting on Complaints [1].

Every NHS Trust has a statutory duty to:

❖ have a designated Complaints Manager (though not necessarily with that title);

❖ have a member of the Trust board who has ultimate responsibility for complaints;

❖ respond within a certain time.

Patients are encouraged to make their complaint as soon as possible, which must be within six months of the event, or within six months of realising that they have something to complain about (but within 12 months of the event itself). These time limits can be waived if there are good reasons why the patient could not complain sooner.

Who can complain?

A patient, or someone on behalf of a patient, but only with their consent. The next of kin of a patient who has died may also complain, or any other relative with the consent of the next of kin.

To whom do patients complain?

Wherever possible they should complain to someone close to the cause of the complaint, for example the doctor, nurse, receptionist, etc. In many cases it is possible to sort out the problem straight away. Every effort should be made by staff to deal with problems at a local level and to resolve issues early, so that patients or carers do not feel the need to resort to a formal complaints procedure.

However, they may prefer to contact the appropriate Complaints Manager, whose telephone number should be readily available. The Patient's Charter gives patients the right to a full and prompt written reply from the Chief Executive to any written complaint against a Trust or Health Authority. The NHS tries to do this within four weeks of receiving any complaint and where there are delays the complainant should be kept informed of progress.

When complaints raised verbally remain unresolved, complainants will be encouraged or assisted to express the complaint in writing. Relevant staff must be notified without delay and responses from an appropriate clinician or clinical manager provided within seven working days of the request.

❖ Procedures for making complaints must be well publicised and easily accessible.

❖ Clear performance targets to ensure a speedy response must be monitored.

❖ Representation for the complainant should be encouraged, e.g. Community Health Council.

❖ Confidentiality of all complaints must be maintained.

❖ A response from the Chief Executive or nominated Deputy must be provided for formal complaints.

What cannot be dealt with by the complaints procedure?

The following cannot be dealt with under the NHS complaints scheme:

❖ complaints about private treatment;

❖ complaints about Local Authority Social Services;

❖ events requiring investigation by a professional disciplinary body;

❖ events about which the complainant is already taking legal action.

105

Table 1.

Overview of Complaints Procedure

1. A patient complains (either within six months of the event, or within six months of knowledge that there may be grounds for complaint).

2. Every effort is made to deal with the matter immediately by those who are involved, for example doctors, nurses, receptionists.

3. If an oral complaint is not resolved, the complainant is encouraged to put it in writing.

4. The Trust must have a designated Complaints Manager.

5. There are national guidelines and local procedures with recognised standards of response times.

6. Ideally there should be Local Resolution by discussion with the complainant and in the presence of a helper, such as a Community Health Council representative and the relevant clinicians, nurses, etc. Written records must be kept of all meetings.

7. Lay Conciliation is an option to resolve a complaint without resort to a Review Panel.

8. **An Independent Review Panel.** The decision whether to proceed with this rests with the Complaints Convenor - a non executive director of the Trust Board - in conjunction with a lay chairperson appointed by the NHS Executive.

9. **The Ombudsman.** When a Panel has been refused or the complainant remains dissatisfied with the outcome of the Panel, they may refer the complaint to the Ombudsman.

Local Resolution

Wherever possible the patient will be given a full explanation, and an apology if appropriate. If something has gone wrong an explanation should be given of steps being taken to prevent the problem from happening again, demonstrating that the Trust is taking appropriate action. If the complainant is still dissatisfied he must be made aware of the second stage of the NHS complaints procedure and the support available to pursue his complaint.

Where it is felt that a meeting between the complainant and staff would be helpful, this should be arranged. This may be before a written response or on occasions after the response to allow the complainant to clarify any outstanding issues. The complainant should be invited to bring a friend or relative and be informed about the role of the Community Health Council. During 2002, depending on legislation, Community Health Councils may be replaced by new arrangements, when a patient advocacy and liaison service (PALS) will be available in all NHS Trusts.

A written record must be kept of any meeting and this must be agreed with the complainant.

The written response to the complainant should have the following features:

❖ the complainant should be thanked for his letter;

❖ the tone must be empathetic;

❖ jargon must be avoided and medical terms explained in simple language;

❖ all issues raised must be addressed with an expression of regret where appropriate, and details of any action taken to prevent a recurrence;

❖ the further options for the complainant, such as an Independent

Review and the role of the Community Health Council must be included;

❖ this final response must be checked for accuracy and agreed with relevant clinicians, (medical, nursing and all of the staff who provided statements or information).

Lay Conciliation

Conciliation is an option to pursue in an effort to resolve a complaint without resorting to an Independent Review Panel. The Conciliator will remain impartial and attempt to reconcile the two parties. The process involves obtaining the views of complainant and staff, followed by a meeting between all concerned, chaired by the Conciliator. This should be completed within four weeks of agreeing to proceed to Conciliation.

If Conciliation is unsuccessful, the complainant can still proceed to a Review Panel.

Independent Review Panel

An Independent Review Panel is normally made up of three people - a lay Chairperson, the Trust Convenor and an additional lay person nominated by the appropriate health authority. Independent clinical assessors may be needed where appropriate and they will investigate issues of specific concern, identified by the Convenor; i.e. terms of reference.

The designated Complaints Convenor, who is usually a non executive Director of the Trust Board will, in conjunction with a lay Chairperson appointed by the NHS Executive, consider the request for a Review. The lay Chairperson should be independent of the Trust and should not be an NHS employee. The Convenor and the Chair will require access to the patient's medical records and it is therefore necessary to obtain consent from the patient, or when the patient is deceased from the next of kin. Where there is a clinical aspect the Convenor will seek independent clinical advice. When all matters have been reviewed, the Convenor, after consultation with the lay Chair, will decide whether or not a Panel should be set up. The decision should be conveyed to the complainant and relevant clinicians or manager within 20 working days of receipt of the request for a Panel.

The Convenor will not proceed with an Independent Review Panel if any of the following apply:-

❖   if the complainant is already taking legal action;

❖   if disciplinary proceedings are under way for the same part of the complaint;

❖   if the same part of the complaint has been referred to a professional body, such as the GMC, an NHS tribunal or the police.

The Convenor may recommend the use of a lay Conciliator with the involvement of local clinicians in order to try and achieve a local resolution. If this is unsuccessful the complainant may still subsequently resubmit his request for an Independent Review Panel.

The Panel will investigate the issues of specific concern identified by the Convenor and agreed with the lay Chair. These are the "terms of reference". The complainant will be invited to attend for interview accompanied by a friend, relative, member of the Community Health Council, or other appropriate representative. Relevant clinical staff will be interviewed. When the Panel has concluded a report will be prepared stating the outcome, the conclusion, and any appropriate recommendations for the Trust to consider. The report should be circulated in accordance with NHS guidelines [2] within 12 weeks of the Panel. Following receipt of the report the Chief Executive will write to the complainant informing him of any action taken concerning the recommendations made by the Panel.

If the complainant is still unhappy he may refer the complaint to the Health Service Ombudsman, whose address is:- The Health Service Ombudsman for England, Millbank Tower, Millbank, London, SW1P 4QP.

There is also nothing to stop any complainant at this stage from seeking legal redress through the courts, which would normally start by an approach to a solicitor.

Summary

The aim of the new NHS Complaints Procedure is to introduce a simpler system with two stages; internal investigation followed by a Review Panel if required.

Disciplinary matters will be considered outside the Complaints Procedure.

The lessons learned from complaints should be used to improve the quality of service to patients, and to satisfy the concerns of the patient/complainant.

References

1. Acting on Complaints - Government Proposals. 1995. In response to: Being heard - the report of a review committee on NHS Complaints Procedures. Health Circular DO16/BH/10M HSSH JO32708. London. Department of Health. 1994.
2. The Audit Commission. What Seems to be the Matter. In: Communication between hospitals and patients. Audit Commission Publications. 1993.

Further Reading*

1. Pickersgill D, Stanton T, Eds. Making sense of the NHS complaints and disciplinary procedures. Radcliffe Medical Press 1997.

---

*   All books appearing in this list do not necessarily reflect an endorsement by the named authors or the publisher.

Chapter 16

The Health Service Ombudsman

A study of the dictionary will show that the word "Ombudsman" is derived from the Norse language, meaning the "King's Man", or "administrator". It is defined as "an official empowered to investigate individual complaints of bureaucratic injustice". The first Ombudsman was appointed in 1973 and initially his remit was to investigate maladministration or failure to provide services within the NHS. However, in 1996 [1] his jurisdiction was extended to include complaints about the exercise of clinical judgement and other complaints about the health services. In addition he can investigate complaints by healthcare workers who feel they have been unjustly treated by the NHS complaints procedure. The change in his powers came at the same time as the introduction of the new NHS complaints procedure.

The NHS Ombudsman is appointed by the Crown and is completely independent both of the NHS and the Government, but is required to make an annual report to a Select Committee at the House of Commons.

The Ombudsman can investigate complaints about hospitals or community health services relating to:

❖ poor service;

❖ failure to purchase or provide a service you are entitled to receive;

❖ maladministration - such as:

- avoidable delay;
- not following proper procedure;
- rudeness or discourtesy;
- not explaining decisions.

❖ not answering your complaint fully and promptly;

❖ complaints about care and treatment provided by a doctor, nurse or other trained professional;

❖ also complaints about family doctors or dentists, pharmacists or opticians providing an NHS service locally.

The complaint to the Ombudsman should be made no later than a year from the date of the events causing the complaint. This time limit can be extended only if there are special reasons. It should also be pointed out that the complainant does not have an automatic right to either an Independent Review or an investigation by the Ombudsman. Leaflets are available explaining how patients go about writing to the Ombudsman together with a complaint form.

Decision

If the Ombudsman decides not to investigate a complaint the reasons will be explained.

When an investigation takes place the Ombudsman will:

❖ review all documents, interview the relevant staff and complainant;

❖ obtain clinical advice before reaching a decision;

❖ prepare a report for circulation to the Trust or Health Authority concerned and the complainant;

❖   make recommendations and monitor follow-up action;

❖   not recommend damages;

❖   make the decision on a complaint which is final, with no appeal.

In an investigation by the Ombudsman, not only is it essential that the medical notes have been kept well, but also that a detailed record is kept at every stage of the complaints procedure.

References

1.   Complaints - Listening, Acting, Improving. Guidance on implementation of the NHS Complaints Procedure. Department of Health. 1996.

Chapter 17

Alternative Dispute Resolution (ADR) including mediation

Alternative Dispute Resolution (ADR) incorporates any method of resolving a dispute between parties except by going to court. In principle it can include: a negotiated settlement by lawyers; mediation; arbitration and/or expert determination. Conciliation is a term often used interchangeably with mediation and arbitration. In this book it is intended to refer only to the process incorporating the NHS complaints procedure. It has no place in situations where litigation is contemplated.

Mediation

In mediation both parties engage the help of a neutral third party to resolve their dispute by negotiation. Both sides meet in a neutral and confidential environment. The meeting rarely lasts more than one day (although it is possible to sit late into the evening!) Advisors, including medical experts, may attend, but are there only to support the parties. No agreement can be made without the consent of both parties, and the content of any mediation is strictly confidential for the purposes of any further litigation (if the mediation proves unsuccessful).

The mediator's role is to assist the participants to reach their own solution to the dispute between them. The procedure will usually be determined by the mediator, but often starts with a joint session in which the parties set out their position. They are then separated, with the mediator going backwards and forwards between them. The objective is to clarify issues and reduce tension.

❖ Mediation is voluntary.

❖ The procedure is informal and private.

❖ There are no strict rules of evidence or procedure.

❖ Mediation is confidential, without prejudice and non-binding unless and until both parties agree otherwise. It is risk-free.

❖ In the event that no acceptable agreement is reached, the parties are free to start (or continue) with litigation.

The mediator is commonly a lawyer, but it should be emphasised that mediation does not replace the need for independent legal advice. Both parties should make all necessary enquiries and investigations, and obtain expert evidence where appropriate, and they must be in a position to make a proper assessment of their own case. If one party has legal assistance and the other does not, the latter is at a distinct disadvantage.

Mediation can be a cheap, informal and (because the atmosphere is less tense) successful form of resolving disputes. Nothing which is said, and no document produced as argument, during the mediation can be referred to in any subsequent trial if mediation does not succeed. When devising the Civil Procedure Rules, Lord Woolf was very keen for litigants to try alternative dispute resolution. By **CPR Rule 26.4** a party may ask for the claim to be stayed (so that the procedural timetable is paused) pending an attempt at ADR. The Court may also make such an order on its own initiative.

Arbitration

Arbitration is not common in clinical disputes. Arbitrations are covered by the Arbitration Act 1996. In essence the parties create, by agreement, their own court. An arbitrator is agreed by the parties (or appointed by a neutral third party in the event of disagreement), whose determination is binding on both sides and can be enforced in court. The parties may agree the procedure for an arbitration and the powers to be provided to the arbitrator. The whole procedure is usually much quicker and cheaper than going to court. The decision can only be appealed in very limited circumstances (such as unreasonable conduct by the arbitrator). Whilst an arbitration clause is common in commercial (in particular construction) contracts, it is very rare in clinical negligence claims.

Expert determination, like arbitration, is (infrequently) used in commercial disputes. Essentially, by agreement, a single expert is appointed to determine the dispute. Its use in medical claims is unheard of.

Further Reading*

1. Lance d' Ambrumenil P. Mediation and arbitration. Cavendish Publishing 1997.
2. Liebman M, Ed. Mediation in context. Jessica Kingsley Publishers 2000.
3. Achieving benefits through mediation: personal injury disputes. The Stationery Office Books 2000.
4. Newman P. Alternative dispute resolution. CLT Professional Publishing 1998.
5. York S. Practical ADR handbook, 2nd Ed. Sweet and Maxwell 2001.

* All books appearing in this list do not necessarily reflect an endorsement by the named authors or the publisher.

PART V

The Surgeon

As Defendant

C h a p t e r   1 8

Litigation: from adverse outcome to trial

Any adverse outcome is capable of resulting in further action from the patient. Often a full explanation (and an apology) will be sufficient. The first notification of a possible impending claim is likely to be either (i) a complaint or (ii) a solicitor's request for the notes. A surgeon may be sued in respect of private work, in which case he should contact his defence organisation immediately for advice. Alternatively, a surgeon may be involved in a case which is brought against his NHS Trust/Health Authority, in which case the complaints/litigation/risk manager will contact the surgeon for his views. Clinical governance requires surgeons to monitor adverse outcomes at the time they occur (all responsible surgeons will be doing so anyway) and consider all the reasons for any particular adverse outcome.

This section is written unashamedly from the point of view of a lawyer who seeks an easier life if and when a legal action is eventually commenced. It deals with a typical civil claim for damages for alleged clinical negligence.

Complaint/request for notes after adverse outcome

In both of these circumstances a response will be required from the surgeon. If the patient (or his lawyer) makes the approach in respect of work carried out privately, the surgeon should immediately seek the advice of his defence organisation. A surgeon who has not kept his defence organisation subscription up to date will be personally liable for the patient's costs and damages in respect of private work and should, first, kick himself and, secondly, seek legal advice immediately (for which he will have to pay). If the approach is made to the NHS Trust/Health Authority in respect of NHS work, the Trust's lawyers will protect the surgeon's interests (but there is nothing to prevent the surgeon seeking advice from his defence organisation in any event). Either way, the patient's complaint/request for notes should be answered formally, usually by the healthcare provider's lawyer.

When a patient commences a legal action for damages, the defending lawyers will need to take an early view as to whether the action is defensible. It is difficult to do this if the surgeon involved has, at the stage of the complaint/request for notes, dashed off a quick memorandum along the lines "no negligence here... outrageous for patient to write in these terms... I am considering making a claim for libel ..." What the lawyer needs is a brief analysis of the surgeon's involvement (including, where they are difficult to read, a transcript of the medical records), the reasons for taking (or failing to take) any particular step and suggestions as to whether the adverse outcome is due to any fault. It is perfectly appropriate for a surgeon to set out the facts and indicate that he will stand by an expert opinion if commissioned (and he may also quite properly suggest expert(s) who may be able to help. Good friends of the surgeon may not always be the most appropriate experts). The sooner this exercise is completed after the adverse outcome, and the more detail it contains, the easier it will be for a lawyer to understand subsequently.

Letter of claim

This letter represents a further step down the road to litigation: it should be drafted by the patient's lawyer and should include details of the proposed claim. The defence lawyer should always seek the surgeon's comments on it. Although the letter of complaint will not always represent the way the claim will eventually be put, it is often the first reasonably detailed indication of the allegations which are to be made. The surgeon should read the letter carefully and comment, so far as possible, on the allegations. It may be that the surgeon recognises a weakness in his actions which has not been picked up on by the patient or his lawyer. The safest course is for the surgeon to bring any such weakness to the attention of his lawyer/employer as soon as possible. The surgeon's answer will be privileged (protected from disclosure), so it need not be sent to the patient.

Particulars of claim

By this stage, the litigation process has well and truly commenced and the surgeon is likely to be faced with yet another request from his lawyer/employer for information. It should be obvious now that the more information the surgeon provides at an early stage, the less onerous is his task at the stage when proceedings are commenced. As is suggested above, the claim is likely to be set out in more detail now, and the surgeon should comment on the detailed allegations of negligence, so that the lawyer drafting the defence has some information on which to work other than guesswork. It is surprising how many doctors subsequently complain about poor drafting by lawyers, forgetting the paucity of the information they provided at the earlier stages of the claim. At about this time the surgeon is likely to meet the solicitor handling the claim to go through the details with a view to drafting a witness statement.

There is no doubt whatever that requests for information on a claim, proposed or actual, impose an enormously heavy time burden on surgeons. No professional likes to see his conduct criticised, let alone falsely so. Some surgeons continue to hide their head in the sand when a claim is intimated; most now take the view that litigation is a fact of life and that, for better or worse, a full answer will eventually have to be given.

Conference

The time has now been reached when the surgeon is invited to a conference (legal terminology for meeting) with the **barrister** handling the defence. Some barristers will prepare a written agenda or plan for this meeting. All will have some idea of the questions and issues they wish to consider. Most forget that this is an important and anxious time for the surgeon whose conduct is criticised. Here are some important (if obvious) hints for surgeons attending conferences:

❖ it is important to leave the conference having understood everything the barrister has said, and his reasons. The next time you see him may be at the door of court on the morning of trial. If in doubt, ask for clarification;

❖ barristers are (usually) expert lawyers. They are not expert doctors. If the barrister has clearly not understood the medicine/surgery involved in this case, explain it to him;

❖ the surgeon's views about the claim are important (but they are not necessarily decisive, whether for or against. The defence organisations and the NHS Trusts/Health Authorities have interests other than the surgeon's to consider). The lawyers need to know the surgeon's views - explain them;

❖ the barrister may well wish to consider whether the claim can and should be settled, in view of the litigation risks. This can be done without any admission of liability. Ask the barrister to explain in full his reasons why early settlement should be considered;

❖ the defence organisations provide helpful literature on all stages of the litigation process. They are there to help, so profit from their experience.

From conference to trial

Many surgeons complain that litigation is conducted without their input and argue that they should be told about what is going on during the course of a case. Good solicitors will now do this as a matter of course. No important decision will (or should) be taken about the case without consulting the surgeon involved. However, there is nothing to stop the surgeon periodically asking for an update from the solicitor handling the defence (though bear in mind that the wheels of justice, whilst they have been recently oiled, are still a little slow).

The surgeon is likely to be asked to comment, in order, at the following subsequent stages of the claim. (At any stage, it is important for the surgeon to tell the lawyers if it appears that any witness has made a mistake or any witness has disclosed information which leads him to change his view).

❖ Witness statements (firstly, his own and those on his behalf before they are exchanged with the other side and; secondly, the other side's witness statement(s) after exchange).

❖ Expert reports (as above, those on his behalf and then the other side's).

❖ **Schedules of Loss** and Counter-Schedules. These documents set out (and respond to) the patient's claim for damages and sometimes include claims for items which are inconsistent or exaggerated. The surgeon's views are welcome.

❖ **Skeleton arguments**. These documents are sent to the trial judge just before the trial starts. They should be the final proof that the barrister has understood the meaning and effect of all the helpful information the surgeon has told him to date. Sometimes, however, they are not. If the opportunity arises, the surgeon should ask to see the Skeleton Argument, particularly if it sets out any detailed aspects of the medicine/surgery involved.

Chapter 19

What happens in court

The surgeon should attend court in good time (asking his solicitor for directions to the court building and to meet him outside if necessary). A surgeon should wear what he would wear to work (or for an interview). The surgeon should ask his solicitor (or defence organisation representative) to show him around the courtroom itself. Now is the time to ask the barrister any questions which the surgeon forgot to ask him at the conference. It is always sensible to bring a pen and some paper (to make notes of the evidence during the trial).

During the conference, the barrister will have asked questions about most of the areas which will be in issue during the trial (though he is not allowed to coach a witness as to the answers which should be given). No-one can fully prepare anyone for cross-examination from the other side's barrister, but the following (again obvious) hints may be useful:

❖ make sure any answers are given at a speed which the judge can make a note of (particularly if they are good answers);

❖ speak up and speak clearly. A mumbling witness is unconvincing;

❖ call the judge by the appropriate title (check with the lawyers beforehand); likewise the patient's barrister (and, ideally, one's own);

❖ if you do not hear or understand a question, ask the barrister to repeat it or clarify it;

❖ if you cannot remember the events in question, do not make an answer up (as this can usually be found out by first-year law students). Do say that you cannot remember;

❖ your barrister should object to any inappropriate question on your behalf. If you have any doubts, ask the judge for guidance;

❖ finally (and most difficult) try to remain calm, at least on the exterior. Anecdotes of witnesses losing their temper are legion amongst lawyers and always reflect badly on the witness.

Chapter 20

The impact

of

being sued

In portraying the "negligent" surgeon the press often conjures up the image of a man lacking in sympathy and care; one who is lazy and irresponsible; who deals badly with people; and whose motives are selfish. This kind of portrayal may occasionally be true, but it is the exception rather than the rule. The majority of surgeons who are sued are well-intentioned and dedicated practitioners: they would neither have embarked on their careers nor achieved promotion if they were not. Indeed, it has been estimated that every doctor can expect to have legal action started against him on at least two occasions in his professional lifetime.

The personal burden

The emotional impact on the surgeon of a serious adverse event is profound, especially when there is any suggestion or feeling that personal error may have been involved: a subsequent claim for negligence intensifies this distress. Different, but equally strong emotions can result from being sued by a patient for whom one has "sweated blood" and gone to great lengths to help, but who then decides to embark on legal action because of an unsatisfactory outcome. Whatever the underlying cause, the burden of a medico-legal claim can result in lack of confidence, sleepless nights, and impaired relationships both with colleagues and patients at work, and with the family at home. Some doctors eventually "lose their nerve", burn out, or seek solace in alcohol or drugs [1]. Sadly, the most sensitive, reflective, and caring personalities are often worst affected by the pressures of being sued.

When the surgeon is not found culpable

Many claims turn out to be groundless, or else they may be dropped by the claimant. While this outcome is clearly a relief to the surgeon, it only happens after he has suffered the emotional assault of accusation; gone to considerable lengths to provide details of the case; and lived with the knowledge of a medico-legal threat hanging over him (often for a long time). The belief that a claim is completely unjustified can cause great anger and frustration.

Another outcome (which most surgeons find disturbing) is settlement out of court by their Trust, with payment of a sum of money to the claimant without any admission of negligence. This causes wounded pride, and many surgeons feel that they have been "sold out". They believe that such payment carries an implication of guilt, and would prefer that such claims should be contested, so that they (the surgeons) are fully and publicly exonerated.

All these emotions and beliefs are understandable - any assault on a surgeon's competence or professionalism is deeply wounding. However, surgeons in the United Kingdom must try to change the way in which they view legal claims, by believing and taking comfort from the following thoughts:

❖ medico-legal actions are now part of our "way of life" in a society obsessed with blame and compensation;

❖ lawyers need to make a living, and will take on any case which appears reasonable (even if they decide later that it is not);

❖ in the NHS they are not sued personally, but are simply named in claims against their Trust;

❖ trusts have to be "hard nosed" financially, and often prefer to pay out small sums of money (without admitting negligence) rather than mounting a potentially costly defence. They may lose money even if they win in court, because their defence costs cannot be retrieved;

❖ claims hardly ever go to court;

❖ most claims cause negligible adverse publicity.

The impact on a surgeon's practice and career

The surgeon who is successfully sued will usually feel that his "proven negligence" is constantly on the minds of those around him. He fears that it will impact disastrously on his referral practice, on his relationships with colleagues, and on the respect in which he is held. In the occasional high profile case, or when gross negligence was involved, then these fears may be borne out. In most cases, however, the effects are negligible and the whole business is quickly forgotten (except by the surgeon himself). The surgeon who generally conducts himself well, and who is known to practice competently as a rule, will receive more sympathy than censure from his professional colleagues. It is very important for surgeons to realise this: a single medico-legal case punctuating years of good practice should have no important and lasting effects apart from the emotional scars.

When a medico-legal claim helps to expose consistently poor practice, operating outside areas of expertise, isolationist behaviour, or dealing unkindly with patients, then the situation is quite different, and ought to result in pressure to change. Unfortunately, these characteristics are often paralleled by lack of insight. It is in this kind of situation that clinical governance should come forcefully into play. While governance is starting to make its impact in the NHS, it is still not easy in the private sector to impose changes of practice on those whose performance and insight are both poor.

Action against a surgeon by the GMC is likely to have more important and far reaching effects on his career than a medico-legal action: this is considered further in Chapter 27.

Action by employers

Quite apart from their natural concern for the safety of patients and quality of care, there are now other powerful motives for chief executives and medical directors of NHS Trusts to take action when a surgeon is accused or found guilty of negligence. First is the spectre of adverse publicity (especially in the wake of the Bristol cardiac surgery case), and second is the mandate of clinical governance that hospitals should learn from adverse events (clinical governance is dealt with in Chapter 14). Concern about disciplinary action by employers worries many doctors; but if a medico-legal claim is an isolated event in the otherwise satisfactory clinical practice of a surgeon, then he should receive nothing but support and help from the managers and legal advisors of his hospital.

When a claim is obviously associated with gross negligence, or when it illuminates a record of questionable practice, then employers need to take action. This action may involve:

❖ discussing aspects of practice with the surgeon, and agreeing limited changes (for example improved counselling of patients, or giving them written information on risks);

❖ agreeing that the surgeon will stop undertaking specified types of work;

❖ agreeing on "re-training" (which may take many forms - from attending a few study sessions or a clinical course; to spending several months being retrained in detail);

❖ recognising health problems (including alcohol or drug problems) which need to be addressed through the occupational health system;

❖ suspension from duties (but it is to be hoped that managers avoid using this potentially damaging step as a "knee jerk" reaction to problems).

It is much more difficult for remedial action to be taken in the context of private practice, where surgeons are self employed; where it is almost impossible to audit their practice; and where they simply have practice privileges at the hospitals where they work (rather than being employees, as in the NHS). When a surgeon is sued in private, there may be negligible impact on the hospital where he operated, and so there may be little or no incentive for the managers of that hospital even to discuss the matter with him. It is possible for private hospitals to suggest the kinds of action listed above, but they are generally inexperienced in this regard, and their only real threat is to remove practice privileges (which might then be strongly contested). By and large governance in private hospitals is as yet an uncharted sea.

Some surgeons fear that if their Trust is successfully sued because of a "breach of duty" on their part, this may count against them in the future. One specific concern is a possible negative effect on the award of discretionary points or distinction awards ("merit awards" - which provide increased salary for a consistent record of extra work). However, these are awarded on the basis of a whole range of activities (clinical, management, leadership, teaching, research, and publication) and the chances of an otherwise hardworking and deserving surgeon ought not to be compromised.

Medical insurance premiums

Unlike motor insurance companies, medical defence societies have neither "no claims bonuses", nor any financial penalties for being successfully sued: an award of damages against a doctor does not affect his annual subscription. "Weighting" of premiums is based only on specialty (related to degree of financial risk) and on level of income. If one of its members were found guilty of very serious negligence, or if he were sued repeatedly then the society might "invite him in" for a discussion to examine his practice and suggest (or demand) changes.

The stance of the defence societies may change in the future, with the introduction of practice restrictions or financial penalties for doctors found guilty of negligence, but these possibilities are as yet only the subject of conjecture and discussion.

References

1. Wu AW. Medical error: the second victim. *BMJ* 2000; 7237: 726-7.

PART VI

The Surgeon

As Expert

Chapter 21

The duties

of

an expert

An expert witness is able to provide opinion evidence (unlike witnesses of fact) on matters which are outside the Court's knowledge. The following list of the duties of an expert were set out by Cresswell J in National Justice Compania Naviera SA v Prudential Assurance Co Ltd ("The Ikarian Reefer") [1993] 2 Lloyd's Rep 68:

❖ expert evidence presented to the Court should be, and should be seen to be, the independent product of the expert uninfluenced as to the form or content by the exigencies of litigation;

❖ an expert witness should provide independent assistance to the Court by way of objective unbiased opinion in relation to matter within his expertise. An expert witness should never assume the role of advocate;

❖ an expert witness should state the facts or assumptions on which his opinion is based. He should not omit to consider material facts which could detract from his concluded opinion;

❖ an expert witness should make it clear when a particular question or issue falls outside his expertise;

❖ if an expert's opinion is not properly researched because he considers that insufficient data are available then this must be stated with an indication that the opinion is no more than a provisional one. In cases where an expert witness who has prepared a report could not assert that the report contained the truth, the whole truth and nothing but the truth without some qualification that qualification should be stated in the report;

❖ if, after exchange of reports, an expert witness changes his view on the material having read the other side's expert report or for any other reason, such change of view should be communicated (through legal representatives) to the other side without delay and when appropriate to the Court;

❖ where expert evidence refers to photographs, plans, calculations, analyses, measurements, survey reports or other similar documents, these must be communicated to the opposite party at the same time as exchange of reports.

In clinical negligence cases, having regard to the <u>Bolam</u> test, an expert witness should make it clear if, although he would have adopted a different practice, he accepts that the practice adopted by the doctor accused of negligence was in accordance with a practice accepted as proper by a responsible and logical body of medical opinion skilled in the relevant discipline [1].

An expert who is perceived by a court to have failed to take adequate account of the above will find himself the subject of (occasionally forthright) criticism from the judge [2].

The impact of the Civil Procedure Rules 1998

An explanation of the origins and reasons for the introduction of the Civil Procedure Rules 1998 is contained in Chapter 8.

Part 35 of the **Civil Procedure Rules 1998** sets out the circumstances in which the Court will allow expert evidence to be given in a case. Any expert who proposes to draft an expert report for use in court must be familiar not only with the substantive law (see Chapter 22) but also with the **procedural law** concerning experts, set out in **CPR Part 35** and its **Practice Direction** (and should ask for a copy from the instructing solicitor in case of any doubt). See also Appendix II. Experts should also be aware of the Draft Code of Guidance for Experts under the CPR, which will eventually become a fully fledged Practice Direction. **Part 35** does not affect the duties of an expert set out above, but builds on them.

In particular CPR **Rule 35.3** states:

(1) *It is the duty of an expert to help the court on matters within his expertise.*

(2) *This duty overrides any obligation to the person from whom he has received instructions or by whom he is paid.*

So important is this provision that CPR also provide for the contents of the expert report (**CPR Rule 35.10**), which include a declaration that the expert understands his duty to the Court and that he has complied with it.

Expert evidence in court

❖ The parties have a duty to restrict expert evidence to that which is reasonably required to resolve the case (**CPR Rule 35.1**).

❖ No party may call an expert to give evidence, or put an expert report before the court, unless the Court has given permission to do so (**CPR Rule 35.4**).

❖ A party who fails to disclose an expert report may not use it at the trial without the court's permission (**CPR Rule 35.13**).

Single joint experts

One of the most controversial changes brought about by the CPR was the power to require that expert evidence be given by a single joint expert (**CPR Rule 35.7**). This power is in fact rarely used in clinical negligence cases, particularly in the crucial areas of breach of duty and causation.

Doubt about the expert's duties and questions about the expert report

Where an expert is in any doubt about his role or duties, he may file a written request to the Court for directions to assist him in carrying out his functions. He need not give any notice to the party instructing him before doing so (**CPR Rule 35.14**). In practice of course an expert facing any such difficulty would be wise to ask his instructing solicitor for assistance before filing such a written request. A party may now put written questions to the other side(s)' expert, the answers to which shall be treated as part of the expert's report (**CPR Rule 35.6**).

References

1. Sharpe v Southend Health Authority [1997] 8 Med LR 299.
2. eg, Rhodes v West Surrey & NE Hampshire Health Authority [1998] Lloyd's Rep Med 246.

Chapter 22

Writing reports

There are a number of different reasons why you may be asked to write a report and the layout and format differs considerably for each. The following types of report may be requested:

1. Coroner's Report

2. Police Report
   a) Witness of Fact
   b) Expert Witness in Criminal Cases

3. Witness Statement as Defendant

4. Personal Injury Report, as Independent Expert Witness

5. Report on Clinical Negligence, as Expert Witness

Each of these will be considered in turn.

1. Coroner's Report

This is a purely factual report from the doctor or surgeon who was most involved with the care of the patient. In the case of the death of a hospital patient it will most commonly be the consultant in charge of the patient.

The statement should include:

❖ full name, qualifications and address of the doctor;

❖ full name, address and date of birth of the deceased;

❖ a detailed summary of the past medical history with dates;

❖ a detailed account of the recent history of the illness or events leading to death.

A doctor should expect, if called as a witness, to be asked for an expert opinion on the issue arising. However, a doctor can only be expected to give an expert opinion on those matters in which he is regarded as an expert.

2. Police Report

a) Witness of Fact

As the doctor who looked after the patient, you must give an account of what happened, both as you remembered it and as recorded in the case notes. This kind of report is normally requested for a patient who has been the victim of an assault. The consent of the patient is needed and you will require relevant clinical notes.

There is a standard form provided by the police for a report of this kind, which may be hand written but it is better to have it typewritten. The report should include:

❖ your full name and qualifications with a brief indication of the experience you have, e.g. consultant, general surgeon for 10 years;

❖ the full name and date of birth of the patient must be given with exact times and dates wherever possible;

❖ include as much detail as possible to avoid being called to court subsequently as a witness of fact.

There is a standard fee for such reports which must be claimed. The police will advise you about this.

b) Expert Witness in Criminal Cases

This is likely to be needed where there is disagreement between the complainant (the patient) and the assailant as to the way in which the injury has occurred. The defendant's legal team may approach you as an independent medical expert. If you are approached you must decide whether the issues are within your field of expertise and also ensure that there is no conflict of interest, e.g. the patient being treated by a friend or colleague.

❖ If you agree to prepare the report you should write to the solicitor confirming this and advising on your likely fee, based on an hourly rate, but pointing out that this might need to be more if the case proves more complex, in which case you will inform the solicitor. You should ideally give an estimate of the time it would take to prepare the report once you have been in receipt of the full instructions and documentation.

❖ You will need the consent of the patient and all relevant medical and nursing records and witness statements of all those involved, plus transcripts of recorded interviews will all need to be studied. All documents studied should be listed and in addition any further documentation that has not been made available.

❖ The format should be similar to that for the witness statement, stating your full name, qualifications, age, etc., and also the name and date of birth of the patient.

The burden of proof in a criminal case is that of "beyond reasonable doubt", which means "almost certain" and is discussed in more detail on page 28. Whereas in civil cases it is "on the balance of probabilities", which means more likely than not, or a greater than 50% chance of.

You should go through the history, clinical findings and investigations, treatment and medical course. Explain each injury in non technical terms. Opinions should be kept separate from facts. It is important that your opinion should be evidence based, i.e. that the diagnosis should fit with the history and physical signs and investigations. While it is good to quote references for the type of condition being discussed, you should nevertheless give your *own opinion* on *this particular patient*.

Remember that the report is prepared for the Court and you should not take sides, but give an impartial and helpful opinion.

3. Witness Statement as Defendant

The initial approach will usually take the form of a solicitor's letter to a hospital administrator, unless it is a private patient, in which case it will be written direct to you. Usually the allegation is made against the hospital concerning a patient under your care. Occasionally you may be named as an individual.

Initial reactions include anger, panic and a temptation to ignore the letter and pretend that you never received it! You should not indulge the luxury of such emotions for long but remind yourself that nowadays only those who are doing no work will be free from such attacks. Remember that help is always close at hand in the form of the hospital legal adviser, trusted colleagues, or in the case of private patients your professional indemnity insurance scheme.

You will need to look through the case notes carefully, see where your involvement lies and answer each allegation appropriately. If you really feel you were at fault you are better to "come clean" and settle early, rather than fight what may be a prolonged battle which you are doomed to lose.

❖ Assuming that you feel that the allegations were unfounded then you must answer each allegation giving clear reasons why you think they are wrong.

❖ Since the Woolf Reforms a blanket denial is no longer acceptable and each allegation must be answered clearly and logically.

❖ Normally the legal advisers to your health care organisation will try to help you as an individual as well as the organisation, but you should remember that their primary responsibility is to the organisation which employs them. If there is a possibility of a conflict of interest between your reputation as an individual and corporate responsibility you may need to seek independent legal advice about the contents of your statement before sending it. (See also Chapter 20).

In conclusion the case notes must be studied carefully and each accusation answered thoroughly and logically. You must not send your report direct to the solicitor for the claimant, but let your legal advisors read and approve it first.

4. Report on Personal Injury

Here you are being asked to act as an independent expert witness. The claimant (patient) will have approached his solicitor, who will write to you. The solicitor will want to know whether you have appropriate specialist experience and they may also ask how often you have accepted instructions from claimants and defendants.

It is essential that you read the solicitor's letter carefully and that you only accept the case if it is within your field of expertise. You should ascertain what you are being asked to give an opinion on, who is instructing you and whether you are being asked as a single or joint expert. You need to obtain all relevant clinical records and the consent of the patient to disclose them and you need to ascertain whether you need to examine the patient.

Having decided to accept the case you must then lay out your terms and conditions of service with details of your anticipated fees based on an hourly rate, also stating the cost for conference or for attending Court and any travelling expenses that may be incurred (fees are dealt with in

145

Chapter 26). Terms and conditions must be agreed prior to agreeing to write the report.

It is helpful to solicitors and the courts if the layout is along the lines suggested below:

History
Numbering each injury and its treatment, preferably in order, head, face, neck, chest, abdomen, spine, limbs.

Present Complaint
Giving each injury and their effect on working abilities, housework, sport, hobbies, etc.

Past History
Any previous symptoms in the injured areas.

Physical Examination
All injured areas,

Xrays & investigations
Include photographs

Opinion and Prognosis
The same numbering as used in history, giving likelihood of permanent problems later and the chances of having to finish work early.

It is also helpful to state whether the length of time off work was reasonable or not, and the length of time symptoms from the accident should take to settle.

The opinion should then be given and the same comments apply as for Expert Witness in a criminal case, see Page 143.

A suggested layout of a medical report is given in Appendix III.

In writing the report:

❖ good quality A4 paper should be used;

❖ the front page should have the name, address and date of birth of the patient, instructing solicitor and their reference, date of the accident, date of report and whether it is the initial or a subsidiary report. If appropriate it should also state the date and place of the first consultation;

❖ each page should have details of the case at the top plus a page number;

❖ it should be typed in either 1½ or double space with margins wide enough for written comments;

❖ there should be a contents page;

❖ there should be an introduction and summary of instructions;

❖ the date of the accident and details surrounding it should be given along with a factual and chronological account of subsequent events;

❖ details should include all the various injuries and subsequent progress;

❖ any relevant past history should be given, both positive, and where relevant, negative, for example where the patient complains they have developed some complication since the accident, it is important to check that they did not already have this condition prior to the accident;

❖ the effect on work, on hobbies, sports, and other social activities should be given. This is a particularly important part of the report and one that is perhaps not always answered as well as it should be;

❖ the opinion should then be given and should be kept separate from the facts;

147

❖ then a final summary may be given;

❖ a standard declaration and statement of truth is required;

❖ a brief (one page) CV giving experience and qualifications should be attached (some people prefer to put this at the beginning of the report);

❖ an appendix of documents examined may be given with copies if they are particularly important;

❖ also references, again with copies of particularly important ones and any photographs, diagrams, etc. should be included.

There should then be a separate covering letter stating your fee. At one time it was customary to give further comments in the letter that were not considered appropriate to put in the main report. This should no longer be done as all material may be disclosed to both parties. In any case the report is written for the court and should not be taking sides

5. Report on Clinical Negligence as Expert Witness

You will normally receive a letter from a solicitor, asking if you would be prepared to act as an expert witness in a case of alleged clinical negligence.

In order for a claimant to prove that a doctor or surgeon was negligent they must show that:

❖ there was a duty of care;

❖ there was a breach of that duty of care (liability);

❖ damage resulted as a direct result of that breach of duty of care (causation).

If any of these three cannot be established then the claim will fail.

The Bolam test is relevant here and it has been discussed on Page 29. The Bolitho test asking whether it was logical to do the operation is also relevant, see also Page 29.

If a patient is treated in hospital there is not usually any problem in establishing a duty of care, so that this is very rarely contested.

The description of the injury suffered by the claimant may be similar to those suffering for example a road accident. The part of the report which establishes whether there is liability is completely different.

Having received such a letter from a solicitor you should read it thoroughly and must try to decide:

❖ whether you are being asked to give an opinion on liability, causation, or both;

❖ whether it is within your field of expertise;

❖ whether you are likely to have a conflict of interest because you know one of the parties well;

❖ in addition to understanding the clinical issues you will need to have a basic understanding of the legal process.

Once you are happy that you can give such a report then your terms and conditions need to be set out in exactly the same way as for a report for personal injury.

Once again it is important to establish the facts as written in the various case notes. In addition to hospital notes you may need to get the General Practitioner's notes, in particular to establish any past history. The layout of the report will be very similar to that for personal injury, with the opinion being kept separate from the facts.

149

In defining the standard of care, the key questions on which the case is likely to be decided involve the <u>Bolam</u> and the <u>Bolitho</u> tests:

❖ Was this operation or treatment that which a responsible body of opinion would have done?

❖ Was it done to the standard which a responsible body of medical opinion would expect?

❖ Was it done for logical reasons?

It will be necessary to have evidence from the literature to support your views, whether you feel the treatment was up to standard or fell short of the expected standard. It may be that the treatment or operation complained of is unusual and not done by you personally. However, if it is described in the literature and the author has found satisfactory results, this should be stated. The treatment does not have to be done to the very highest standards, but to a standard reasonably expected of a competent surgeon. That is the benchmark against which it will be judged.

Having written the whole report the expert should give a summary of the facts including the opinion.

Further Reading*

1. Foy MA, Fagg PS, Eds. Medico-legal reporting in orthopaedic trauma. Churchill Livingstone 1996.

* All books appearing in this list do not necessarily reflect an endorsement by the named authors or the publisher.

Chapter 23

Using the published literature as evidence

What is, and is not, reasonable and common practice may be determined in a number of ways, and the role of the expert witness in this process is considered in other chapters within this part of the book. The published literature is a fundamental source of information, and is used by medical experts, lawyers and courts to determine whether the actions of doctors were reasonable, as part of the Bolam principle. However, the way that the literature is used and interpreted can have an important influence on the conclusions which are drawn.

The nature of "evidence" from the published literature

In considering use of the literature as "evidence" it is first helpful to remember the very different meanings of this word for the medical and legal professions. Lawyers relate evidence in civil cases to a balance of probabilities, using a threshold of greater or less than 50% to decide whether a premise is "true" or "false" (while in criminal cases evidence must prove a point "beyond reasonable doubt"). Doctors now recognise "levels of evidence" from the published literature, in descending order of importance and certainty, as follows:

❖   evidence from good randomised controlled trials;

❖   evidence from non-randomised trials;

❖ evidence from cohort or case studies;

❖ evidence from multiple time series, opinions of authors, etc.

Unfortunately, this understanding of the strength of evidence in medical practice may not be fully understood by those involved in judging the actions of doctors, and there is endless scope for expert witnesses to present evidence from the literature selectively (and persuasively) if they wish to do so.

The bias of the published literature

The published literature almost always portrays results better than average, and this may be a serious problem for the surgeon who is accused of substandard practice. There are several reasons for this bias:

❖ surgeons usually choose to publish their results only if they seem particularly good, and to hide them if they are poor (in addition, there are numerous ways in which authors can "enhance" their results [1]);

❖ large published series often originate from big specialist centres, where results are better than average;

❖ there are strong motives relating to patient referral and financial gain in publishing good results in many parts of the world (for example in the United States, but less so in the United Kingdom);

❖ editors and reviewers of medical journals generally favour articles describing good results, and tend to reject submissions describing average or poor results: this applies particularly to the major, world class journals (whose articles are most often used and cited).

All this means that the results of the average surgeon will, as a rule, compare poorly with those which experts can cite from the literature. This fact may devalue the presentation of good audit data as part of a medico-legal defence (discussed earlier on).

Systematic reviews

These have become very influential in recent years, because they can provide thorough and balanced appraisals of the current evidence on any area of medical practice. It is therefore important that lawyers and judges understand their implications, especially if they are countered by experts citing selectively from the literature, or from their own personal experience. In areas where sufficient studies of high quality exist, systematic reviews (often using the technique of **meta-analysis**) can demonstrate clearly whether or not an intervention is effective. An example is the effectiveness of aspirin in preventing cardiovascular events [2].

By contrast, it is also important to recognise when the conclusions of a systematic review are tentative, or offer only a partial answer. The use of patches in **carotid endarterectomy** is an example [3]: overall, the outcomes with patch closure are better than those without, but uncertainty persists about the influence of carotid artery diameter and other factors. It would be wrong to use these inconclusive systematic review data against a surgeon who had not used a patch.

Registries and collated data

Surveys, and use of centrally collected data (for example from hospital information systems) are other means of elucidating common practice and outcomes, which often differ from those found in published trials and studies. They may be criticised for imperfections and potential incompleteness of data, but they provide some evidence in the medico-legal arena for typical everyday practices and results. It is, however, worth noting that:

❖ hospital information systems in the U.K. have a reputation for inaccuracy [4];

❖ voluntary registers are likely to contain deceptively good results, because some people will not submit their bad ones;

❖ registers compiled by non-voluntary data capture may produce poorer results, because they may include inappropriate cases, and make no allowance for **casemix**.

Questionnaires and surveys

There has been a glut of questionnaires about all kinds of aspects of medical practice, and many doctors have a low threshold for consigning any postal questionnaire to the dustbin. The value of questionnaires is reduced by poor design and poor response rates (indeed, any conclusions are suspect with a response rate of <60%, and largely valueless with a response <50%). Nevertheless, questionnaires can provide valuable published evidence about common practice by "a responsible body of medical opinion", and some questionnaires have been designed specifically with this purpose in mind. Two examples in vascular surgery are as follows:

Varicose veins and venous thromboembolism (VTE) [5]. Varicose veins are the commonest condition for litigation against general and vascular surgeons, and VTE is a potentially serious and costly cause of medico-legal claims after varicose vein operations. There are widespread misconceptions about the relationship between varicose veins and VTE, enhanced by national [6] and international [7] consensus documents, which list varicose veins high among the risk factors for VTE. There is, in fact, no evidence at all that varicose vein surgery carries a particularly high risk of VTE, and in the mid 1990s many surgeons did not use specific **prophylaxis** against VTE for varicose vein operations. Nevertheless, the popular misunderstandings and influential consensus documents might well have conspired against a surgeon who had not used prophylaxis and whose patient had suffered VTE.

A questionnaire was sent to all members of the Vascular Surgical Society of Great Britain and Ireland (VSSGBI) asking surgeons about their views and practices relating to varicose vein operations and VTE prophylaxis [5]. Eighty percent responded, of whom only 12% always used subcutaneous **heparin** VTE prophylaxis, and 17% never did so. The remainder used prophylaxis selectively, and responded to questions about the factors which influenced their patient selection. These data could provide considerable support for a surgeon facing a claim of negligence, for instance, by a previously fit patient who had **unilateral** varicose vein surgery without heparin prophylaxis. Conversely, the responses confirmed that almost all surgeons would use heparin prophylaxis for a patient with a history of VTE, which is in tune with good published evidence, and which would properly add to the case against a surgeon who had failed to do this. As a result of the high response rate by colleagues, this questionnaire provides a good medico-legal reference source, as intended by the author.

The second example concerns ruptured aortic aneurysms, and the decision not to operate on some patients [8]. This issue has seldom been addressed in detail, and offers scope for complaint or legal action if a patient is denied operation. The response rate of 81% testified to the interest with which vascular surgeons viewed this subject, and their responses have provided a sound foundation of data justifying selective treatment as normal practice, and including age as an important influence on this decision (54% of surgeons would seldom or never operate on patients over 85). Three quarters of surgeons would seldom or never operate on patients with severe neurological disease (for example advanced Parkinson's disease); cardiac pulmonary, and renal disease were influential factors for the great majority of surgeons; and residents in long term care (for example in a nursing home) influenced all but 13% (with 34% stating that they would seldom or never operate on such patients). Interestingly, medico-legal considerations only ever influenced 22% of surgeons in the decisions they made. These data provide sound evidence about the views and practice of "a responsible body of medical opinion" regarding operation for ruptured aortic aneurysm, and should lend support to any surgeon facing a complaint or claim about failure to operate on such a patient because he felt that surgery was not in the patient's best interests.

References

1.   Campbell B. Interpreting the literature. In Ed. Campbell B. Complications in arterial surgery: a practical approach to management. Oxford. Butterworth Heinemann. 1996. pp 205-13.

2.   Antiplatelet Trialists Collaboration. Collaborative overview of randomised trials of antiplatelet therapy - I: Prevention of death, myocardial infarction, and stroke by prolonged antiplatelet therapy in different categories of patients. *BMJ* 1994; 308: 81-106.

3.   Counsell CE, Salinas R, Naylor R, Warlow CP. A systematic review of the randomised trials of carotid patch angioplasty in carotid endarterectomy. *Eur J Vasc Endovasc Surg* 1997; 13: 345-54.

4.   Whates PD, Birzgalis AR, Irving M. Accuracy of hospital activities analysis operation codes. *BMJ* 1982; 284: 1857-8.

5.   Campbell WB, Ridler BMF. Varicose vein surgery and deep vein thrombosis. *Br J Surg* 1995; 82: 1494-7.

6.   Thromboembolic Risk Factors (THRIFT) Consensus Group. Risk of and prophylaxis for venous thromboembolism in hospital patients. *BMJ* 1992; 305: 567-74.

7.   European Consensus Statement. Prevention of venous thromboembolism. London. Med-Orion. 1992.

8.   Hewin DF, Campbell WB. Ruptured aortic aneurysm: the decision not to operate. *Ann R Coll Surg Engl* 1998; 80: 221-5.

Chapter 24

Experts'
discussions

❖ Where each party has its own expert(s), the Court has power to direct a discussion between experts of like discipline (**CPR Rule 35.12(1)**). Such discussions are often referred to as "meetings", although there is in fact no requirement that the experts meet face to face. The discussions commonly take place over the telephone, though this does not accord with the **Clinical Disputes Forum** guidelines (see below).

❖ The Court may (and invariably does) also direct that a report be prepared of the areas on which the experts agree and disagree, and the reasons for such disagreement (**CPR Rule 35.12(3)**). The content of the discussion itself (as opposed to the report which results from it) may not be referred to at the trial unless the Court gives permission.

❖ Two documents for guidance exist: the Draft Code of Guidance for Experts Under the Civil Procedure Rules 1999 (awaiting approval by the Vice-Chancellor) and, more importantly for this book, the draft Guidelines on Experts' Discussions in the Context of Clinical Disputes (see Appendix IV), published by the Clinical Disputes Forum, a cross-interest body. These latter will be referred to as the "CDF draft Guidelines". It should be noted that the guidelines produced by the Clinical Disputes Forum are draft guidelines only, and at present they have no approval from any other body.

When should a discussion between experts take place?

Only a small proportion of cases (probably not more than 5%) in which an expert's advice is sought actually end up going to court. In many cases it is the discussion between the experts which persuades the parties of the strengths and weaknesses of their case, and leads to eventual settlement without the need for trial. Frequently the experts will be able to agree in certain points and, if not, to narrow the areas of dispute. Patients are often acutely suspicious about the experts' discussion (since the parties themselves will rarely, if ever, be present). They will need to be reassured strongly that everything has been done as fairly as possible. It follows that the experts' discussion is an extremely important stage of the litigation process.

In practice a discussion between experts will not usually take place until each expert has prepared an initial report and the parties have exchanged their expert reports. A fuller explanation of the litigation process is set out in Chapter 8 which should also be read in conjunction with Chapter 19. There is nothing to prevent the expert from requesting a discussion with his opposite number, although this should always be discussed (out of courtesy) with his solicitor first.

Advance preparation for the experts' discussion

❖ The expert should make sure he has all the relevant information. The CDF draft Guidelines state:

"5(3) The experts should be provided with the following documents before the discussion: (a) the medical records; (b) if proceedings have been issued, the statements of case, the claimant's chronology, the defendants' comments on the chronology, the witness statements and the experts' reports as exchanged; (c) if proceedings have not been issued then the parties should agree a chronology and provide this to the experts with witness statements and such experts' opinion as has been exchanged."

❖ The expert should also make sure that there is an agreed agenda for the discussion. Usually this will have been prepared and agreed by the lawyers for each side. The CDF draft Guidelines state:

"5(1) There must be a detailed agenda. Unless the parties agree otherwise, the agenda should be prepared by the claimant's lawyers (with expert assistance) and supplemented by the defendants' lawyers, if so advised, and mutually agreed. The agenda should consist as far as possible of closed questions, that is questions which can be answered "yes" or "no". The questions should be clearly stated and relate directly to the legal and factual issues in the case."

❖ It is prudent to stick fairly rigorously to the agreed agenda. However, the Court has power to specify the issues which the experts must discuss (**CPR Rule 35.12(2)**). An expert can raise any issue which he believes to be relevant and could, in an extreme case, ask the Court for guidance. In practice, discussion with the lawyers in advance will usually avoid problems.

How to conduct the experts' discussion

❖ The CDF draft Guidelines state:

"5(2) The discussion should take place face to face or by video link. Exceptionally, and having regard to proportionality, the discussion may take place by telephone. Save in exceptional circumstances these guidelines (and in particular paragraph 6 below) should apply whatever the form of the discussion."

❖ It is important to remain calm, to listen to the other expert and to keep an open mind during the discussion. The other expert should always be treated as a colleague of equal merit.

❖ It is also important not to bully or attempt to pull rank on the other expert.

❖ Whilst an expert should not be defensive or back down without good reason, it is important not to be unnecessarily dogmatic. An argument should always be supported with reasons and evidence.

❖ Both experts should keep a note of their discussion (important for the agreed report at the end).

❖ The agreed report should accurately reflect the conclusions of the meeting. The CDF draft Guidelines state:

"6(A) At the conclusion of a face to face discussion a statement must be prepared setting out: (1) A list of the agreed answers to the questions in the agenda; (2) A list of the questions which have not been agreed; (3) Where possible a summary of the reasons for non agreement; (4) An account of any agreed action which needs to be taken to resolve the outstanding questions in (2) above; (5) A list of any further material questions identified by the experts, not in the agenda, and the extent to which they are agreed or alternatively, the action (if any) which needs to be taken to resolve these further outstanding questions. Individual copies of this statement must be signed by all the experts before leaving any face to face meeting.

(B) Before the conclusion of a discussion at a distance, identical statements setting out all the information required in paragraph (A) above must be prepared and signed by each expert. Unaltered signed copies must be exchanged immediately."

❖ An expert will have to be prepared to justify any change of opinion to his client and solicitor, remembering of course that he (unlike the lawyer) owes his overriding duty to the court and not to the client.

Should lawyers attend the experts' discussion?

There is some disagreement about whether lawyers should attend the experts' discussion. Perhaps surprisingly, the CDF draft Guidelines expect that lawyers will usually attend. In practice this is unusual. If a lawyer does attend the experts' discussion (in order to maintain his client's confidence in the litigation process) his input should be restricted to:

❖ assisting the expert on any relevant question of fact or, more likely, law;

❖ preventing the experts from inappropriate discussion;

❖ taking a note of the discussion (in order to assess with his client the real effect of expert debate).

CHAPTER 24

Chapter 25

How to become

an

expert witness

Initially the best thing is to go on a course on how to be an expert witness, such as those run by Bond, Solon Training, although there are many other courses and most are well advertised. It is worth getting your name in the directories of expert witnesses, the Law Society Directory, the Register of Expert Witnesses, or to join a professional association such as the Expert Witness Institute.

It is also worth going through the local "Yellow Pages" and writing to all the solicitors in your area informing them that you are available for giving reports and giving details of your areas of expertise, a brief CV and your likely fee.

Other methods are to speak to the local law society, give talks to groups of lawyers, either in their own practices or in conferences and to write articles in professional press and legal journals about your special interest.

It is worth having a brief CV with your areas of expertise available to give at short notice. In addition your availability over the coming months is also helpful, as are details of the cases that you have acted for over the previous months or year or two.

Since the Woolf Reforms and the advent of a single joint witness, solicitors are less likely to make a direct approach, but may use an intermediary company, which keeps a list or "Expert Panel", for the various specialities. In order to get on this expert panel you will need to advertise by writing to them with all your details. The names and addresses of such companies known to the author are given in Appendix V. Some of them will ask for a fee in which case you should check at the end of a year as to whether the fee was justified by the work they brought in.

If you give a good service, giving clear, sensible, balanced reports, written within the time that you have said, then word of mouth will result in more work.

Chapter 26

What to charge

for an

expert report

Coroner's Report

This is a duty for which there is no fee.

Report As A Defendant

This is also a duty for which there is no fee.

Police Report

a) Witness of Fact

There is a standard, fairly modest, fee, which the police who requested the report will advise you on. However if you do not ask and put in a claim they may not pay you automatically.

b) Expert Witness

Either for the police in personal injury, or in a clinical negligence claim, you must establish your fees along with other terms and conditions before embarking on the report. In addition it is important to establish who will be responsible for these fees. It is better to avoid conditional fee agreements (i.e. no win, no fee). In any case this would be improper because the doctor is not supposed to take sides, but the report should be to the court and therefore entirely independent.

For a straightforward personal injury report most solicitors prefer a fee for the report which would normally be in the region of £250. If it is more complicated and lengthy, then it is better to give an hourly rate, perhaps between £120 and £130 per hour at the time of writing this book. These rates are suggested as being suitable for someone starting as a medical expert, but many people charge considerably more than this, particularly if they are an established authority on the subject of the report. You may be given an upper limit to which you can go, particularly in cases involving public funding.

Having given your estimate, if there is a lot more evidence to look through than you had realised and it is obviously going to take significantly longer than you thought, you should then inform the instructing solicitor that there will be an increased cost. The possibility of this happening should be established prior to accepting that you will do the report.

If there is a report from another medical expert that requires reading and responding to, the time taken for this should also be recorded and charged for and similarly this possibility should be established prior to giving the report.

It is unwise to agree to wait for the case to be settled before getting your fee. You should establish that your fee will be paid within a certain time limit, e.g. 60 days.

What to do if payment is delayed

If the fee is not paid within the specified time, then initially a reminder should be sent. Acrimony should be avoided as you may be hoping to do further work for the solicitors; a letter of complaint to the senior partner is the next step.

If the fee is still outstanding you may write to the solicitors threatening to report them to the Office for the Supervision of Solicitors (the body which has succeeded the Solicitors Complaints Mechanism).

The threat itself may suffice, but if this fails, then one can write to the Office for the Supervision of Solicitors at: Victoria Court, 8, Dormer Place, Royal Leamington Spa, Warwickshire, CV32 5AE.

PART VI - Further Reading*

1. Tsushima WT, Nakano KK. Effective medical testifying: a courtroom handbook for physicians. Butterworth Heinemann 1998.
2. Cato DM, Ed. The expert in litigation and arbitration. LLP Professional Publishing 1999.
3. Holburn C, Solon M, Bond C, Burn S. Healthcare professionals as witnesses to the Court. Greenwich Medical Media 2000.
4. Bond C, Leppard J. Marketing for the expert witness. Bond Solon Publishing Ltd. 1996.
5. Bond C, Solon M, Harper P. The expert witness in court - a practical guide. Shaw & Sons 1999.

*   All books appearing in this list do not necessarily reflect an endorsement by the named authors or the publisher.

PART VII

The GMC
and
The Coroner

Chapter 27

The General Medical Council (GMC)

The General Medical Council (GMC) is constituted according to the law set out in the Medical Act 1983 and is the body which regulates the medical profession in the UK. Its purpose is to protect the public from medical practitioners who are inadequately trained or whose standard of care falls short of that expected of the profession. The GMC have clearly set out the duties of a doctor registered with them [1]:

"Patients must be able to trust doctors with their lives and well-being. To justify that trust, we as a profession have a duty to maintain a good standard of practice and care and to show respect for human life. In particular as a doctor you must:

❖ make the care of your patient your first concern;

❖ treat every patient politely and considerately;

❖ respect patients' dignity and privacy;

❖ listen to patients and respect their views;

❖ give patients information in a way they can understand;

❖ respect the rights of patients to be fully involved in decisions about their care;

❖ keep your professional knowledge and skills up to date;

❖ recognise the limits of your professional competence;

❖ be honest and trustworthy;

❖ respect and protect confidential information;

❖ make sure that your personal beliefs do not prejudice your patients' care;

❖ act quickly to protect patients from risk if you have good reason to believe that you or a colleague may not be fit to practise;

❖ avoid abusing your position as a doctor; and

❖ work with colleagues in the ways that best serve patients' interests.

In all these matters you must never discriminate unfairly against your patients or colleagues. And you must always be prepared to justify your actions to them. For further information on how to apply these principles, please read our booklet 'Good Medical Practice'[1]."

The Members of the GMC

There are 104 members. These are made up of:

❖ Elected members, 54 doctors elected from four constituencies; England, the Channel Islands, and the Isle of Man; Wales; Scotland; and Northern Ireland.

❖ Appointed members, 25 doctors selected by universities, medical schools and other bodies which are able to award medical qualifications and can lead to registration.

❖ Nominated members, 25 lay (non-medical members) who represent the public and are nominated by the Privy Council.

A President is elected from amongst the members of the GMC.

There are seven statutory committees which carry out regulatory functions required under the Act. These are:

❖   The Preliminary Proceedings Committee.

❖   The Professional Conduct Committee.

❖   The Health Committee.

❖   The Education Committee.

❖   The Assessment Referral Committee.

❖   The Committee On Professional Performance.

❖   The Interim Orders Committee.

Functions of the GMC

The main function of the GMC is to give doctors their licence to practise medicine in the United Kingdom. Their motto is "To Protect Patients And Guide Doctors"; this is done by:

❖   promoting good medical practice;

❖   keeping an up-to-date register of qualified doctors;

❖   promoting high standards of medical education;

❖   taking action if there are doubts about whether a doctor should stay on the register.

Legal powers

The GMC has been given legal powers by Parliament [2]. These powers cover doctors in all branches of medicine including hospitals and general practice; and apply to their work both in the NHS and private practice.

They can investigate any complaint received, provided it raises a question about a doctor's registration, whether it is from a member of the public, from another doctor or from public authorities, such as Health Authorities or Board, an NHS Trust or the Police.

They can take action if they find any of the following:

❖ the doctor has been guilty of "serious professional misconduct" (this is conduct which questions whether a doctor should be allowed to continue to practise medicine without restriction);

❖ the doctor has been convicted of a criminal offence in the British Court (or convicted abroad of an offence which is also an offence in the U.K.);

❖ the doctor's professional performance is "seriously deficient" (they are repeatedly failing to meet the standards expected of doctors in their professional work);

❖ the doctor is seriously ill and this is affecting their ability to practise.

The action may range from a reprimand to restricting or removing the doctor's right to practise medicine. However the GMC is not able to award compensation. Only the Courts can do that. The GMC is currently undertaking a fundamental review of its procedures. This chapter describes the procedures as they stand.

Serious Professional Misconduct

The GMC refers to this as being "behaviour which calls into question whether a doctor should be allowed to continue practising medicine without restriction" [3].

In order to determine the standards expected of a doctor, regard will be given to the GMC publication "Good Medical Practice" [1]. Examples provided by the GMC of conduct that could lead to a finding of professional misconduct are [4]:

1. Serious neglect or disregard of professional responsibilities to patients.

2. Certifying as true, information which the doctor knows to be untrue or has not taken appropriate steps to verify.

3. Improper charging of private fees to NHS patients or false claims on the NHS.

4. Any other form of dishonesty.

5. Abuse by the doctor of their position of trust, including a breach of a professional confidence.

6. Any form of indecency or inappropriate sexual conduct towards a patient or colleague or any other person.

Mental and physical health

If a doctor's practice is seriously affected by ill health then the GMC will investigate and may remove the Practitioner's registration or put conditions on his practice in order to protect patients. The GMC has reported that most referrals are for mental illness and alcohol or drug abuse [5].

Professional performance

A doctor's registration may be suspended if there is evidence of seriously deficient professional performance. This is defined as "A departure from good practice, whether or not it is governed by the specific GMC guidance, serious enough to call to question a doctor's registration". This particularly applies if the doctor might be putting patients at risk [6].

175

Examples of problems of performance given by the GMC are [4]:

1. Failure to keep professional knowledge or skills up to date.

2. Failure to recognise the limits of professional competence.

3. Failure to maintain any/or adequate clinical records.

4. Inability or unwillingness to take an adequate history or to perform a competent physical examination.

5. Attempting to practise techniques in which the doctor has not been appropriately trained.

6. Inability or refusal to communicate effectively with patients or their relatives.

7. Failure to work effectively with colleagues.

Complaints

If a patient wishes to make a complaint, they may discuss this with the GMC at any time. It is important to appreciate that the GMC is not a general complaints body. It can deal only with matters which call a doctor's registration into question. Once the decision to make a formal complaint has been made, the complainant should write giving as much of the following information as possible:

❖ the full name and address of the doctor;

❖ details of what, in their view, the doctor has done wrong;

❖ the dates when the events took place;

❖ copies of any relevant papers, and of any other evidence such as tape recordings or photographs;

❖   name and address of anyone else who witnessed the events, who could support the complaint from their own personal knowledge.

The GMC has its own solicitors who can help complainants (e.g. patients) with the legal side of complaints. There is no time limit for making complaints, although the longer the time that passes the harder it may be to get all the relevant details.

The process of a complaint

A patient may complain to the GMC whether or not they have complained to another organisation, for example a Hospital Trust or the Police. Sometimes the GMC wait for other organisations to complete their investigations before taking further action.

All complaints about doctors are taken seriously. Every substantive complaint will first be assessed by one of the GMC "screeners". The "screener" will be a medically qualified member of the GMC who will consider the complaint carefully, looking at the following:

❖   how serious the matter is;

❖   any other information that may have been received about the same doctor;

❖   the information given by the complainant.

If the screener decides that the GMC should take further action, the complainant will need to make a sworn written statement to support his complaint. The GMC may also need written statements from other people with personal knowledge of the events, although these will not need to be sworn statements.

The GMC will not take the complaint further, if:

❖   the complaint is not serious enough to review the doctor's registration;

177

❖ the doctor cannot be identified;

❖ the complaint is about an NHS service where doctors are not involved;

❖ where there is no evidence to prove the complaint and no prospect of obtaining it;

❖ complaints which are not related to a doctor's medical work;

❖ where the complaint is anonymous and cannot be independently verified. Decisions to take no action must be agreed by a lay screener, who represents the public.

Subsequent action

The law gives three ways in which the GMC can tackle problems with doctors. There are three procedures:

❖ The Conduct Procedures

These allow the GMC to deal with cases where the doctor has been convicted of a criminal offence, or has done something which can be seen as serious professional misconduct. If the Committee finds serious professional misconduct, then it may [7]:

1. Erase the doctor from the register. After a period of 5 years the doctor can apply to be put back on the register.

2. Suspend the doctor's registration for up to 12 months.

3. Make registration subject to conditions, such as limiting areas of work. This may last for up to three years.

4. Reprimand the doctor.

A doctor who is suspended may have the suspension renewed for up to 12 months at a time. The suspension can be converted to erasure or conditional registration (again with the three year time limit). A conditional registration may be reviewed for 12 months or revoked in whole or part.

❖ *The Performance Procedures*

Those doctors whose general clinical performance is thought to be seriously deficient. This means that they are repeatedly failing to meet the standards expected of doctors in their professional work.

Under these circumstances the doctor is invited to undergo an assessment of his performance, which is usually carried out by two specialists in the relevant field of medicine or surgery and also a non-medical person. If deficiencies are identified after assessment, the coordinator may decide that the case can be dealt with on a voluntary basis, with the doctor agreeing to restrictions on his practice and to taking remedial action. If, however, the case is more serious, or the doctor does not agree, then the matter is referred to the Committee on Professional Performance.

The Hearing of the Committee on Professional Performance is normally held in private and the doctor may have legal representation. The GMC will instruct lawyers to present the case, and witnesses and other evidence will be called. This Committee can impose conditions on a doctor's registration for three years, or can suspend his registration for 12 months. A suspension may be converted to conditional registration for a maximum period of three years. Any suspension can be made indefinite after a two year period. Such a move is reviewed at the doctor's request after two years and at two yearly intervals thereafter. There is a right of appeal on a question of law to the Privy Council.

❖ *The Health Procedures*

These are used where a serious illness may make a doctor a danger to patients or colleagues. The most common problem has been cases involving mental illness, alcohol abuse or some form of addiction.

What is the difference between the procedures?

The three procedures (above) are different because they are designed to deal with different problems. The Conduct Procedures are similar to a criminal investigation where the doctor is asked to respond to particular allegations. The final stage may be a public hearing which is rather like a trial in the Courts.

The Performance and Health Procedures are concerned with assessments of the doctor's health or day to day performance, rather than the particular event leading to the complaint. Where the investigation finds a serious problem of performance or health, the aim is to get the doctor's voluntary co-operation. For example the doctor might have medical treatment, or may be told to take action to improve his performance. If the doctor does not agree then there may be formal hearings. If it is thought the public is at immediate risk then the case will be referred to a committee. A sick doctor is not allowed to carry on practising medicine unless it is considered safe for him to do so, and he is properly supervised.

Both the Performance and Health Procedures usually take place in private (the doctor may choose for a committee hearing to take place in public).

The Preliminary Proceedings Procedure

If it is decided to take forward a complaint about the doctor's conduct the Preliminary Proceedings Committee (PPC) will review all the papers on the case. These will include the complaint and any comments the doctor has sent in response. After considering the evidence the Committee can do one of four things:

❖ decide the case should have a public hearing before the Professional Conduct Committee;

❖ send the doctor a letter of advice or reprimand;

❖ refer the case for investigation into the doctor's health;

❖ decide no further action need be taken.

The Professional Conduct Committee (PCC)

This Committee will investigate complaints concerning serious professional misconduct. The PCC usually meets at the GMC offices in London. All PCC hearings are in public, although some parts of its proceedings may take place in camera by application of the complainant or doctor. Reporters usually attend and there is frequently quite wide publicity both on radio, television and in the local and national newspapers.

The doctor may be "struck off" (erased from the register) in the most serious cases, but the PCC has a wide range of other options available. For example sometimes the doctor will be given a reprimand; in other cases conditions will be placed on the doctor's registration, limiting the scope of his medical work to make sure that patients are protected. In more serious cases the doctor can be suspended, preventing him from practising medicine for up to a year at a time.

The doctor can appeal to the Judicial Committee of the Privy Council, a panel of Law Lords who are independent of the GMC. The Judicial Committee can quash the PCC's decision, substitute a lesser sanction or refer it back.

It has been pointed out [8] that the GMC's Professional Conduct Committee with the full glare of publicity can have a devastating effect on the professional and personal life of a doctor. There are no restrictions designed to prevent salacious or impressionistic reporting. Such stories have untold potential for damaging a doctor's career, personal and professional reputation and practice before any case against him has been proven. Inappropriate press intrusion adds to the doctor's burden when he is already subject to considerable stress. The obvious solution would be for the GMC to withhold details of a case until a Committee has reached a decision, but at the present time this is not the case.

The Interim Orders Comittee (IOC)

Cases should be referred to the IOC when a doctor faces allegations of such a nature that it may be necessary for the protection of members of the public, or otherwise be in the public interest or in the interests of

181

the doctor, for the doctor's registration to be restricted whilst those allegations are investigated. The IOC may make an order suspending a doctor's registration or imposing conditions upon a doctor's registration for a maximum period of 18 months. The IOC must review the order within 6 months of the order being imposed and, thereafter, at intervals of not more than 3 months. Cases which may warrant referral to the IOC include clinical issues (particularly where there is a continuing risk to patients), non-clinical issues (for example, indecent assault) and cases involving a breach of conditional registration or undertakings to limit practice. Further details are given on the GMC website.

Summary

The GMC is the regulatory body for the medical profession. No doctor may lawfully practise medicine unless he is registered with the GMC. The GMC has the power to erase or suspend the doctor's registration or to impose restrictions on his practice as necessary. The grounds for these sanctions are serious professional misconduct, seriously deficient professional performance or because the doctor's health has seriously impaired his fitness to practise.

References

1. Good Medical Practice. General Medical Council, 178 Great Portland Street, London, W1N 6JE. 1998.
2. Medical Act 1983.
3. A Problem With Your Doctor? How the GMC Deals With Complaints. General Medical Council, 178 Great Portland Street, London, W1N 6JE. 1997.
4. The Management of Doctors With Problems: Referral of Doctors to the GMC's Fitness to Practise Procedures. General Medical Council, 178 Great Portland Street, London, W1N 6JE. 1997.
5. GMC Annual review. General Medical Council, 178 Great Portland Street, London, W1N 6JE. 1998.
6. When Your Professional Performance is Questioned - The GMC's Performance Procedures. General Medical Council, 178 Great Portland Street, London, W1N 6JE. 1997.
7. Medical Act 1983, Section 36.
8. Overexposure: disciplinary proceedings before the GMC and the media. The Journal for Members of the Medical Protection Society. *Casebook* 1999; 14: 5 - 7.

Chapter 28

The

Coroner

Introduction

The main function of the Coroner is to identify the deceased and to discover "where, when and by what means" the deceased came to his death. The Coroner system is inquisitorial, rather than adversarial: in the normal legal forum (a court), there are two sides, but in the Coroner's court everyone with a legitimate interest can ask relevant questions and be legally represented. The Coroner has great autonomy in his own court and the proceedings are controlled by him, sometimes with considerable variation between Coroners. The Coroner is answerable to the Lord Chancellor and his decisions can be scrutinised by the High Court.

Who are Coroners?

Coroners are usually lawyers, but may sometimes be doctors. They are independent judicial officers. Each Coroner has a Deputy and the Coroner or his Deputy is available at all times. Coroners are helped by their officers, who receive reports of deaths and make enquiries on behalf of the Coroner.

When is a death reported to the Coroner?

Under the Coroners Act 1988 the Coroner is required to hold an inquest into deaths where there is reasonable cause to suspect the death was [1]:

❖ violent or unnatural;

❖ sudden or unexpected and of unknown cause;

❖ in prison, or elsewhere in circumstances where an Act of Parliament requires an inquest to be held.

Who reports deaths to a Coroner?

Any of the Police, Ambulance Trust, Registrar of Deaths or doctors (General Practitioner or hospital doctor) may report a death to a Coroner. In addition, if a doctor has not notified the Coroner, the Registrar of Deaths is obliged to do so if [2]:

❖ the deceased was not attended by a doctor in his last illness;

❖ he is unable to obtain a completed death certificate;

❖ the deceased was not seen by the doctor completing the certificate either after death or within fourteen days before death;

❖ the cause of death is unknown;

❖ the death was unnatural or caused by violence or neglect or by abortion or in suspicious circumstances;

❖ the death occurred during or within twenty four hours of an operation or before recovery from the effects of an anaesthetic;

❖ the cause of death was due to an industrial disease or industrial poisoning.

In cases where death is reported to the Coroner's officer the relatives must be told that death cannot be registered until the Coroner has finished his investigation.

It should be noted that any death caused by medical or surgical treatment or its complications is at least initially considered to be an unnatural death and should be reported to the Coroner's officer, even when the treatment was given more than 24 hours before death. In the majority of cases the advice will be that a death certificate can be issued, but this decision is at the discretion of the Coroner.

What will the Coroner do?

❖ The Coroner may decide that death was due to natural causes. Where the Coroner is satisfied that a medical practitioner was entitled to sign a medical certificate of the cause of death, and that there are no other circumstances which require him to become involved, he should inform the medical practitioner (and the Registrar of Deaths), so that the death can be registered on the medical certificate.

❖ The Coroner may ask a pathologist to examine the body. If the examination shows death has been a natural one there will be no need for an inquest and the Coroner sends to the Registrar of Deaths a certificate (Pink Form B) showing the cause of death as disclosed by the post mortem examination.

❖ The Coroner may authorise removal of the organs or tissues for use for therapeutic purposes, education or research [3].

❖ The Coroner may hold an inquest. This usually involves two stages:

(1) *an opening, when the Coroner records in public that a person has died and that a fuller investigation is to be carried out on a later date;*

(2) *the full inquest hearing, when the Coroner hears evidence and gives his verdict (the formal record of the inquest findings, see below). He*

185

will normally begin the formal inquest process as soon as possible after death to permit funeral arrangements to be made, (and then the inquest will, technically, be adjourned).

The Inquest

What is the purpose of an Inquest?

The purpose of an inquest is limited and is to answer four factual questions ("the four questions") [4]:

1. Who was the deceased?

2. When did the deceased die?

3. Where did the deceased die?

4. How did the deceased die?

It is not the Coroner's job to determine any question of criminal or civil liability, (although sometimes it becomes clear from the evidence that there has been negligence). When all the facts about the cause of death are known then any person whose conduct has been called into question may be brought before another court where a claim for damages may be made.

Where a person has been charged with causing someone's death, e.g. by causing death by dangerous or careless driving, or by murder or manslaughter, the inquest is adjourned until that person's trial is over. Any other court proceedings will normally follow the inquest.

The Hearing

The Coroner's court varies considerably from informal to more formal surroundings. The inquest is normally opened by the Coroner's officer, asking those present to stand as the Coroner enters the room. The Coroner will explain the purpose of the inquest and then call the first witness, who will often be a member of the family of the deceased. As it is an inquiry by the Coroner he asks questions of the witnesses, which may include expert witnesses, in order to answer **the four questions**, of which the fourth question ("How did the deceased die?") is usually the main issue.

Other interested parties are also entitled to ask witnesses questions, either by themselves or via a lawyer. A "properly interested person" may be:

❖ a parent, spouse, child or anyone acting for the deceased;

❖ anyone who gains by a life insurance policy on the deceased;

❖ any insurer having issued such a policy;

❖ anyone whose action the Coroner believes may have contributed to the death, accidentally or otherwise;

❖ the Chief Officer of Police, who may only ask witnesses questions through a lawyer;

❖ any person appointed by a Government department to attend the inquest;

❖ any one else who the Coroner may decide also has a proper interest.

Verdict

The following verdicts may be given [5]:

❖ natural causes;

❖ industrial disease;

❖ dependence on drugs/non-dependent abuse of drugs;

❖ want of attention at birth;

❖ suicide;

187

* attempted/self-induced abortion;

* accident/misadventure;

* sentence of death;

* lawful killing;

* open verdict;

* unlawful killing;

* stillbirth.

Neglect/lack of care or self-neglect should not be given as a stand-alone verdict but may qualify as one of the above verdicts (e.g. misadventure aggravated by lack of care).

If the Coroner feels that there is evidence of a serious criminal offence having been committed, he may adjourn the inquest and refer the facts to the Crown Prosecution Service. He also has a duty under the Coroner's Rules to bring to the attention of an appropriate authority circumstances in which death has arisen where action might be taken to avoid similar deaths in the future. This is an important function in modern society.

Jury

Most inquests are held without a jury. There are particular reasons when a jury will be called which include:

* if death occurred in prison or in police custody;

* if death resulted from an incident at work;

* if death occurred on a railway.

In every inquest held with a jury, it is the jury, and not the Coroner, which makes the final decision (this is called returning the verdict).

Medical witnesses

Medical witnesses are not often called to give evidence in person. Their statements are usually accepted as documentary evidence. When the matter is controversial and particularly if the relatives are dissatisfied or if there is a difference of opinion on medical matters, then the Coroner may require doctors to attend the inquest.

Accident/misadventure

The courts have held that there is really no difference between these two terms and that accident or accidental death is the preferred terminology. The difference between natural causes and accidental death can be illustrated with an example of aortic surgery. If a patient is admitted with a ruptured abdominal aortic aneurysm and dies during or shortly after the operation this would be "natural causes". If however a patient has an elective repair of an aneurysm and following the operation the suture line leaks and the patient dies this would be recorded as "accidental death" since the patient would not have died at that time without the operation and, therefore, it was not due to natural causes. However the operation was being performed in order to try and save the patient from dying at a later date.

A verdict of natural causes does not exclude clinical negligence in the care of the patient. Conversely a verdict of accidental death does not imply any clinical negligence either. These matters are outside the remit of the Coroner.

Since the purpose of the inquest is to discover "where, when and by what means" the deceased came to his death, no determination of crime or civil liability is allowed to enter the proceedings. In spite of this where issues of negligence exist lawyers present may probe long and deep into the medical aspects of the case. The doctor must answer with honesty and clarity, and referring to clinical notes when necessary which should have been brought to the inquest.

While it is not always necessary for lawyers to be present, it is sometimes sensible for the medical attendants also to have a lawyer to

189

represent them when there is a question of possible clinical negligence, or when the relatives of the deceased have a lawyer representing them. It is quite common for lawyers to use an inquest to "trawl" for evidence of clinical negligence and to use the inquest to decide whether to institute subsequent civil proceedings. They can only do this if their questioning is relevant as to how the deceased came by his death.

Summary

The Coroner inquires into the circumstances of a death by seeking to find answers to the four specified questions. Although the inquest may raise difficult issues over how the deceased died it is not the Coroner's duty to make any determination of civil or criminal liability.

References

1. Coroners Act 1988, section 8.
2. Registration of Births and Deaths Regulations 1987, reg 41(1).
3. Human Tissues Act 1961.
4. Coroners Act 1988, section 11(5)(b).
5. Coroners Rules 1984, Schedule 4, Form 22, Note (4).

Further Reading*

1. Matthews P. Jervis on Coroners, 11th Ed. Sweet & Maxwell 1993.
2. Matthews and Foreman. Jervis on Coroners: 4th supplement to the 11th Edition. Sweet and Maxwell 1998.
3. Knapman & Powers. Sources of Coroners' Law, 1st Ed. Barrys Rose Law Publishers 1999.
4. Dorries C. Coroners' courts: a guide to law and practice. Blackstone Press 2000.

---

* All books appearing in this list do not necessarily reflect an endorsement by the named authors or the publisher.

Glossaries

Medical glossary

Advance directives (Living wills): formal statements prepared by individuals specifying their wishes with regard to medical treatment: in particular they may state a wish not to receive certain treatments (e.g. blood transfusion) or not to be resuscitated under certain circumstances. May be given to local hospital to be kept in medical records. May be a problem to discover an advance directive in an emergency.

Adverse events: a comprehensive term used to include postoperative complications, and other medical problems which develop during the course of a patient's care.

Aortic aneurysm: a local ballooning of the aorta (referring in this book to the aorta in the abdomen) which is at risk of leaking or bursting: this is rapidly fatal if untreated (less than 50% patients with "ruptured" aneurysms reach hospital alive, and less than 50% who have emergency operations survive).

Audit/Clinical audit: the process of checking whether any aspect of clinical care is being carried out as intended. Introduced as a formal requirement in the NHS in 1989/90. Happens at national and local level. Often involves a number of clinical disciplines, working together. If deficiencies are found they should be remedied, and a further audit then done ("the audit cycle").

191

Bilateral: on both sides of the body (for example bilateral varicose vein surgery means operation to both legs: operation on one leg only is unilateral).

British Medical Association: the main professional society for doctors, and their main political "voice". Membership voluntary by subscription. Diverse professional, educational, and political activities. Publishes books and journals, including the British Medical Journal (BMJ).

Carotid/Carotid endarterectomy: the carotid artery passes up through the neck and takes blood to the eye and the brain. Narrowing of this artery may be the source of blood clots which can cause minor or major strokes or blindness. These may be prevented by aspirin treatment, or by operation to remove the narrowing (endarterectomy): decisions need to balance the risk of stroke with and without each kind of treatment.

Casemix: the characteristics of patients seen or treated by a particular surgeon or hospital. May vary in terms of age, severity of disease, other diseases present, etc. These factors may account for differing results of treatment, despite similar quality of care.

Clinician: this word was formerly used to describe any kind of doctor. It is now often used to describe all kinds of "healthcare professionals" who deal with patients (doctors, nurses, physiotherapists, etc.).

Complication/Complicated: an unwanted or adverse side effect of treatment. Important to remember this implication: a treatment which is difficult or detailed should not be described as "complicated" but as "complex".

Confidential Reports: the reports of national enquiries which retrieve details of selected patients who have died, analyse them, and publish recommendations. The individual data are protected by Crown Indemnity. Include the Confidential Enquiry into Maternal Deaths and the National Confidential Enquiry into Perioperative Deaths (NCEPOD).

CPD (Continuing Professional Development)/CME (Continuing Medical Education): the process of ensuring that doctors (CME) and latterly all healthcare professionals (CPD) receive education and keep up to date with relevant new information throughout their careers.

CNST (Clinical Negligence Scheme for Trusts): the indemnity scheme established in 1995 to insure all hospital Trusts against claims for negligence, in association with the **NHS Litigation Authority (NHSLA)**. CNST inspects all aspects of risk management in Trusts, offering different insurance premiums for "Levels 1-3" of achievement.

Deep vein thrombosis (DVT): see **Venous thromboembolism**.

Defence Society: refers to the three medical defence societies - The Medical Defence Union (MDU), The Medical Protection Society (MPS) and the Medical and Dental Defence Union of Scotland (MDDUS). These provided insurance for all negligence claims against doctors until 1989, and subsequently for all doctors working outside NHS hospital Trusts (in general or private practice). Still offer help for claims within the NHS if requested by members. Subscriptions vary depending on specialty, seniority, and income: all have escalated greatly in recent years.

Dermoid: a type of cyst formed from skin and skin glands during foetal development.

Ductus arteriosus: the blood vessel which allows blood to bypass the lungs in an unborn child. Should close off at birth.

Elective: describes a treatment which takes place at a planned and convenient time, within the limitations of the service, and without any urgency.

Electroconvulsive therapy (ECT): a treatment for severe depression, involving passage of an electric current through the head, which produces a seizure or fit: done under general anaesthetic.

Evidence based medicine: medical treatment in accordance with the best published advice resulting from good scientific studies. The

193

"evidence base" may be analysed by "systematic reviews" which help to define which treatments work by detailed analysis of the published literature (see also Meta-analysis). The Cochrane Collaboration and the U.K.Centre for Reviews and Dissemination are two important organisations which publish evidence based reviews.

Existing Liabilities Scheme (ELS): this funded all claims against NHS bodies for incidents prior to April 1995 and with total costs exceeding £10,000.

Extradural haematoma: a collection of blood between the skull and the brain, caused by head injury. Can lead to unconsciousness and death unless recognised and evacuated by an emergency operation on the skull.

Finished Consultant Episode (FCE): an episode of treatment under the care of a particular consultant in hospital. FCEs are used as an index of hospital activity.

GMC (General Medical Council): the statutory body for the UK which governs the standards of practice and behaviour of doctors. Doctors must be registered with the GMC to practice. There is a separate GMC for the Republic of Ireland.

Health Circulars: letters from the Department of Health dictating policy to the NHS. Each has a specific reference - for example DHSS HC/99/7.

Healthcare Record: includes parts of the record of care of a patient (medical and nursing notes, letters, results of investigations, charts, consent forms, etc.). Now used in preference to "casenotes" or "medical record" (implying doctors' records only). The term Electronic Patient Record is used specifically to describe Healthcare Records held on computer.

Heparin: an anticoagulant drug, which makes the blood clot less readily. It can be given intravenously (into a vein) for immediate effect; but is now more often given subcutaneuosly (beneath the skin) both for the prevention (smaller doses) and treatment (larger doses) of venous thromboembolism.

Incident reporting/Clinical incident reporting: a system within a hospital which enables clinicians to report to management any problems which might lead to a complaint or medico-legal action. Steps can then be taken to limit potential harm, counsel affected patients and relatives, and ensure good records.

Integrated Care Pathway (ICP): a specifically defined plan for the anticipated progress of a patient with a particular condition through the health care system, including the various investigations, treatment, and follow-up required. Designed by agreement between all the disciplines who will care for patients, both in primary and secondary care. Intended to achieve "best practice" and limit variations in the care which patients receive. Brings separate clinical records into a single patient care document.

Intervention: a word used to encompass all kinds of "invasive" treatments, including surgical operations, endoscopies (telescope examinations), and operative treatments under X ray control (for example balloon dilatation of arteries or insertion of stents - by "interventional radiologists").

Intubate/Intubation/Intubated: a term often used specifically to refer to the passage of an endotracheal tube into the trachea (windpipe). This allows the patient to be "ventilated" using either a mechanical ventilator or a bag to pump air (or anaesthetic gases) directly in and out of the lungs.

Ischaemic: adjective describing reduced or absent blood supply to any part of the body (noun - **ischaemia**).

Junior doctor/Trainee: includes all grades of medical staff in hospital apart from consultants (and excluding the permanent non-consultant grades of staff grade, clinical assistant, and associate specialist). Progression is from House Officer ("Houseman" - first year after university qualification, provisional GMC registration only), to Senior House Officer ("SHO" - usually 1-4 years), and finally to Specialist Registrar ("SpR" - for 5-6 years). Trainees are always responsible to a consultant for the care of his patients.

Laminectomy: an operation removing the back parts ("laminae") of one or more vertebrae of the spine. Often done to relieve pressure on the spinal cord or nerves.

Ligation: tying off with a ligature.

Living will: (see **Advance directive**).

Meta-analysis: a statistical method used in systematic reviews for examining the effectiveness of a treatment, based on the combined results of several different scientific studies (see **Evidence Based Medicine**).

Myelogram: a special X ray study of the spine, done by injecting radio-opaque contrast ("X ray dye") into the fluid around the spinal cord.

National Practice Data Bank: a national register in the USA listing medical practitioners for whom "malpractice" payments have been made.

Neurogenic: caused by a disorder of the nervous system.

NHSLA (National Health Service Litigation Authority): established in 1995 to deal with all medico-legal claims against hospital Trusts, with potential liability greater than the Trust's insured excess. Operates in conjunction with **CNST**.

NICE (National Institute for Clinical Excellence): established in 1999 to provide appraisals of new and existing health technologies (drugs, other treatments, etc.); to produce national guidelines (on referrals and clinical practice); and to suggest simple audit methods which can be applied to their guidance at a local level (see **Audit**).

Outcome: word used increasingly to describe the end result of any medical intervention: includes the effect on function and quality of life. May describe either a good outcome (cured, back to normal, happy) or a bad result of treatment (complications, disability, unhappy, dead).

Perioperative: about the time of an operation (cf. preoperative - before an operation; and postoperative - after an operation).

196

Primary care: medical care delivered outside hospital, by general practitioners and associated health professionals.

Prosthetic: man-made. Used specifically to refer to grafts implanted into the body (e.g. prosthetic hip joint. Some types of graft may be either native to the patient (e.g. a length of vein used to replace an artery) or prosthetic (e.g. a polypropylene or polytetrafluoroethylene graft used to replace an artery).

Prophylaxis: used specifically in this book to refer to the prevention of venous thromboembolism, which can be done in a variety of ways (giving heparin injections, prescribing special stockings, encouraging early mobilisation after an operation).

Prostate: gland situated around the urethra (tube carrying urine) just below the bladder in men. Produces part of the fluid component of semen. The prostate often enlarges with age, which causes difficulty in passing urine.

Protocol: a written plan of management for a particular medical condition. Protocols are more specific and are regarded as more "mandatory" than guidelines, so doctors often worry about the medico-legal consequences of departing from a protocol.

Pulmonary embolism (PE): see **Venous thromboembolism**.

Saphenous vein: part of the name of two different superficial veins, under the skin of the leg. The long saphenous vein runs up the inner side of the leg and thigh to join the (deep) femoral vein in the groin (the **saphenofemoral** junction). The short saphenous vein runs up the back of the calf to join the (deep) popliteal vein behind the knee (the **saphenopopliteal** junction).

Stoma: any part of the gut or urinary tract brought purposely to the skin surface: usually covered by a plastic drainage bag to receive intestinal contents or urine. The commonest are a colostomy (part of the colon, which produces faeces, often constructed after operations for cancer)

197

and an ileostomy (part of the ileum, which produces odourless intestinal fluid, often constructed after operations for ulcerative colitis).

Systematic review: see **Evidence Based Medicine** and **Meta-analysis**.

Unilateral: on one side of the body (eg. Unilateral varicose vein operation - operation on one leg only: both legs - **bilateral**).

Venous thromboembolism: describes both the formation of thrombosis (blood clot) in the deep veins of the legs and pelvis (**deep vein thrombosis - DVT**) and also the subsequent dislodgement of the blood clot, which travels through the veins to the heart and thence to the lungs where it lodges, blocking blood vessels there (**pulmonary embolism - PE**). See also **Prophylaxis**.

Glossaries

Legal glossary

Accelerated receipt: damages for **future loss** are **discounted** to reflect the fact that **the award of damages** is payable now for **financial or pecuniary loss** which would not have been incurred until some time in the future.

Action: used interchangeably with **case** and **claim**.

Allocation, allocated: see **tracks**.

Award of damages: the sum of money which a Court orders to be paid to the **claimant** to compensate him for his injury, **loss** and **damage**.

Balance of probabilities: see **standard of proof**.

Barrister: a referral-level lawyer who conducts the **case** at **trial** (when they will wear robes and wigs) and is usually involved at one or more of the following stages: drafting formal documents in the **case**; advising on the strengths and weaknesses of a case; conducting conferences (meetings) with experts and witnesses. **Barristers** must usually be instructed by a **solicitor** and cannot be contacted direct. Also called **counsel**.

Breach of duty: an essential element of **negligence**.

Burden of proof: the party who has the legal duty of proving any issue to the Court bears the **burden of proof** on that issue. A party who fails to satisfy the Court to the requisite degree on any issue has failed to discharge the **burden of proof**.

Case management: the Court now has a duty under the **Civil Procedure Rules 1998 (CPR)** to manage **claims** efficiently, bearing in mind not only the requirements of the case before it, but also the needs of other litigants. Elements of **case management** will include: the need to analyse the main issues in the **case**; a swift determination of non-essential issues; orders for the procedural timetable of the **case**; sanctions where one party fails to comply with the timetable.

Case management conference: a Court hearing at which the procedural timetable is determined. This can be done on paper with the co-operation and agreement of the Court and the parties, and can also now be done over the telephone without the need for lawyers to attend Court in person.

Causation, caused: an essential element of **negligence**.

Citation, cite: for every proposition a lawyer wishes to put forward, he is expected to **cite** some authority. The hierarchy of acceptable authorities is:

Statute/statutory instruments
Previously decided **cases**
Academic (eg, textbooks, legal articles, etc)

Primary legislation (statute) of the UK Parliament is referred to by its short title (usually found in the pre-amble of the Act itself), e.g. the Fatal Accidents Act 1976, the Data Protection Act 1998.

Secondary legislation (statutory instruments) is referred to by its title, e.g. Data Protection (Subject Access Modification) (Health) Order 2000. The Statutory Instrument's reference number is also given, e.g. (for the above) SI 413/2000 (meaning that it is the 413th statutory instrument in the year 2000).

cases are cited by the names of the (principal) parties, separated by "v". When read out, the symbol "v" translates to "and" (out of preference) or "against" and <u>never</u> "versus" or "vee". Law reports are catalogued either by year (in which case the reference will use square brackets) or by number (in which case the year, if desirable to be given, should be put in round brackets). The names of all law reports are abbreviated. The page number then follows. Finally, if desired, the level of court which heard the **case** may be given (HL - House of Lords; PC - Privy Council; CA - Court of Appeal; QBD - Queen's Bench Division; DC - Divisional Court). Thus:

<u>Bolitho v City & Hackney HA</u> [1998] AC 232, HL. This **case** will be found in the Appeal cases for 1998 (which we can tell are: (i) organised by year because of the square brackets and (ii) contain only one volume for the year 1998) at page 232. The **case** was decided by the House of Lords.

<u>Taylor v West Kent HA</u> (1997) 8 Med LR 251. This **case** will be found in numbered volume 8 of the Medical Law Reports at page number 251. It happens to have been decided in 1997.

Some law reports are more authoritative than others and advocates are expected to find the most authoritative version of the **case** they wish to cite. The official law reports rank highest.

The following abbreviations for judges are commonly found (in descending order of seniority):

Ld Smith - Lord Smith (House of Lords or Privy Council)
Smith LJ - Lord (or Lady) Justice Smith (Court of Appeal)
Smith J - Mr or Mrs Justice Smith (<u>never</u> "Justice Smith")
HHJ Smith - His (or Her) Honour Judge Smith (County Court)

Civil Procedure Rules 1998, CPR: the rules which govern the procedural aspects of any **action**. The rules provide a unified set of procedures for the High Court and County Court. They came into force on 19th April 1999.

Claim: action, case.

Claimant: the party who brings the **claim**, formerly **plaintiff**.

201

Claim form: the document which formally commences the **claim**, formerly **writ** (High Court) or **summons** (County Court).

Clinical Disputes Forum: a group of the key people in the field of clinical negligence litigation, working together to try to improve its procedures, and reduce the number of patients who have to go to law to resolve their disputes with their doctors and other healthcare providers. It is currently applying for registration as a charitable company. The Forum originated with the Woolf Inquiry into Access to Justice in 1994-6. Many people, both lay and professional with every possible connection with medical litigation, were consulted in the course of his Inquiry. He then called for the foundation of an "umbrella" organisation of people who would normally never talk to each other but who, as the Inquiry had proved, could work together for the benefit of patients and health professionals alike. The Forum was founded in January 1996.

Clinical negligence: formerly medical **negligence**.

Conditional fee agreement: an agreement between the **claimant** and his lawyer by which the lawyer will not be paid for the legal work he carries out unless the **claimant** is successful and receives an award of damages, in which case the lawyer will receive an uplift (up to 100% depending on the degree of risk involved) on the fees which he would otherwise have charged. (Cf; the US position, where the lawyers are paid a percentage (typically 40-50% of the award of damages.)

Contract, law of: the following elements are required for a valid **contract**: (i) offer; (ii) acceptance; (iii) consideration (usually the payment of money); (iv) the intention to create legally binding relations. A **contract** may be oral and/or in writing. Subject to some practical difficulties of proving an oral **contract**, there is no difference between the two. A **contract** will contain express terms (principally for payment) and implied terms. The terms of a **contract** set out the obligations of the parties to the **contract**. A breach of **contract** may give rise to a **claim** even where there is no **loss** or **damage**, cf **negligence**, though **damages** in such **cases** would only be nominal.

Contributory negligence: a **claimant** may contribute to his own adverse outcome by his own **negligence**. The award of **damages** may be decreased by reason of (and in proportion to) the **claimant's negligence**. **Expert evidence** will rarely be required to prove that the **claimant** was negligent, as the Court will be able to determine this itself. However, there are very few cases of **clinical negligence** in which a **claimant** has been shown to have been **contributorily negligent**.

Costs: refers to the legal **costs** of bringing a **claim** (i.e. lawyer's fees, expert fees, court fees, etc). To be distinguished from **damages**.

Counsel: see **barrister**.

Damages: the sum of money payable to a **claimant** by a Court as compensation. See **award of damages**. To be distinguished from **costs**.

Declaration: a court order which simply sets out (declares) any particular legal situation.

Defence: the document (**statement of case, pleading**) in which a **defendant** answers the **particulars of claim** and explains why he is not liable (or liable only in part) to the **claimant**. Also a general legal term describing a legal principle which, if successful, enables a **defendant** to avoid liability to the **claimant**.

Defendant: the party against whom the **claimant** brings his **claim**.

Disclosure: the procedural term which governs the production of, and subsequent exchange of, relevant documents. Formerly **discovery**.

Discounted, discounting: see **accelerated receipt**.

Discovery: see **disclosure**.

Discretion: the situation where a court is enabled, but not required, to make a certain decision. A discretion must nonetheless be exercised according to legal requirements of fairness (taking into account relevant circumstances, not taking into account irrelevant circumstances, balancing the interests of the parties, etc).

Duty of care: an essential element of **negligence**.

European Convention on Human Rights: the international treaty which now has direct applicability in UK law since the coming into force of the Human Rights Act 1998 on 2nd October 2000.

Evidence: the testimony of a witness. Such **evidence** can either be of fact or opinion. Hearsay **evidence** is the out of court statement of any person which is put forward as **evidence** of the truth of the matters contained in it. The rules against the admission of hearsay **evidence** have been relaxed over recent years, but hearsay **evidence** should always be treated with caution and may be of less weight than the direct oral testimony of a witness in court. **Evidence** can be oral or documentary.

Expert: a witness who is entitled to give **evidence** of his opinion (unlike a witness of fact). See also **single joint expert**.

Floodgates: the **policy ground** which is often raised in an attempt to prevent development of new areas of **negligence**. According to this analysis, if the new development is allowed to occur, the floodgates will open and the Courts will be awash with, and clogged down by, new litigation.

General damages: the element of an **award of damages** which compensates the **claimant** for his **pain, suffering and loss of amenity**.

Hypothetical causation: a term used for one aspect of **causation**, where the Court needs to determine what would have happened in any one hypothetical situation.

Implied term: see **contract**.

Injunction: an order by a Court which usually prevents someone from doing something; very occasionally an **injunction** may order someone to carry out a particular act.

Injury: see **personal injury, personal injuries; pain, suffering and loss of amenity**.

Judgment: the decision of a Court after a hearing, and the reasons for it. Note the spelling.

Judicial Studies Board: The Judicial Studies Board provides guidance for judges on all areas of law. In particular it produces a booklet called "Guidelines for the Assessment of General Damages in Personal Injury Cases". Now in its fifth edition, this booklet was written in an attempt to codify and classify **awards** of **general damages**. It is a highly useful starting point for a lawyer wishing to quantify the **claim**, but is no substitute for proper consideration of previously reported **cases**.

Legal Aid: see public funding. Now, technically, abolished (though the last cases which were granted **Legal Aid** before abolition are now working their way through the system.

Legal Aid Board: see **Legal Services Commission**.

Legal Services Commission: the successor body to the **Legal Aid Board**. Administers **public funding** of appropriate **actions**.

Letter before action: see **letter of claim**.

Letter of claim: the letter by which a **claimant** indicates to a **defendant** that he has grounds for bringing a claim. The requirements of a **letter of claim** are contained in the **Pre-action Protocol, for the Resolution of Clinical Disputes**. Failure to send a **letter of claim** in the required detail may have adverse **costs** consequences at a later stage. Formerly **letter before action**.

Limitation; time-barred; out of time; section 14; section 33: the Limitation Act 1980 provides a specific defence to a **defendant** where a **claim** is not commenced within the prescribed time limit. A **claim** which is not commenced in time is said to be **out of time** or **time-barred**. An **action** which includes a **claim** in respect of personal injury must be commenced within three years of the date when the cause of **action** accrues or the date on which the **claimant** has knowledge of the certain elements of his **claim**. The elements of the **knowledge** which are required are defined in **section 14** of the Act. In addition, the Court has a general **discretion** to disapply the time limit in a personal injury claim even where the **claimant** has started the **action** out of time (see section 33).

Litigation: the process of commencing, prosecuting and resolving legal proceedings.

Loss and damage: used interchangeably, essential elements of **negligence**.

Managing, management: see **case management**.

Material contribution: a legal principle relevant to **causation**, developed to assist **claimants** who would otherwise have great difficulty in proving that the breach of duty caused their **loss** and **damage**. The extent to which the breach of duty must contribute to the **loss** and **damage** before it will be classified as material has not been defined precisely and will always be a matter for the trial judge to decide, assisted by expert **evidence**.

Measure of damages: the term given to the legal principle by which an award of **damages** is calculated. The compensation to which a **claimant** is entitled may depend on which area of law governs the **claim**.

Negligence: the main sub-category of the **law of tort**. The essential elements which a **claimant** needs to prove are: (i) the existence of a duty of care; (ii) breach of duty which (iii) causes (iv) **loss** and **damage**. If the **loss** and **damage** includes an injury, the **claim** will be categorised as a **personal injury action**. Note that however gross a breach of duty, it will not give rise to a **claim** unless it causes **loss** and **damage** (cf **contract**). The categories of **negligence**, i.e. the situations in which a person may be found to have been **negligent**, are never closed.

Offer to settle: according to Part 36 of the CPR, a **claimant** can now offer to settle his **claim** on payment by the **defendant** of a certain sum of money. If the **defendant** refuses the offer and the **claimant** is awarded more **damages** at trial, the **defendant** may have to pay interest at a punitive rate.

Pain, suffering and loss of amenity: the elements of an award of general **damages**. Such an award compensates the **claimant** not only for the injury itself but also for the consequent (non-financial) effects on his life of the injury (e.g. inability to pursue former hobbies, **loss** of sexual function, etc).

Particulars of claim: the document (**statement of case, pleading**) in which a **claimant** explains why the **defendant** is liable to him.

Payment into court: a **defendant** may pay a sum of money into court in full and final settlement of the **case**, without admission of liability. The trial judge will not be told anything about the payment into court. If the **claimant** refuses to accept the payment into court and is awarded a lower award of **damages** at trial, he will pay the **defendant**'s **costs** of the **case** from the date the payment into court was made. The rules governing these payments are set out in Part 36 of the CPR.

Personal injury, personal injuries: a disease or impairment of someone's physical or mental condition.

Plaintiff: see **claimant**.

Pleadings: the general term for the formal documents in which the parties set out the nature of and basis for their **case**. Such documents are intended to set out the **case** in skeleton form, and will not include all the **evidence**, nor, generally, matter of law. See **particulars of claim, defence, statement of case**.

Policy grounds: considerations other than matters of strict law which affect the determination of any issue in a **case**.

Precedent, previously reported cases: where there is no decisive legislation on any point, courts will consider whether there is any "binding precedent". If there is a **case** which appears to deal directly with a point in issue, a court will be bound by (i.e. have to follow) that decision unless it can be distinguished because either it does not on closer examination fully cover the facts of the present **case** or it is wrongly decided. In principle any court will be bound by decisions of a court of higher authority. Thus High Court judges are bound by decisions of the Court of Appeal, which is bound by decisions of the House of Lords. Although in principle the House of Lords is bound by its own previous decisions, it decided in 1966 that it could change its mind if necessary. The Privy Council comprises the same judicial committee which makes up the House of Lords and hears appeals from some Commonwealth countries (and some tribunals, like the GMC). Its decisions are not technically binding on UK courts, but are highly persuasive. The Court of Appeal is bound by its own previous decisions. The High Court will take into account decisions of previous High Court judges and ought to follow them as a matter of "judicial comity". Frequently, however, as new points of law are raised (and, rather like fashion, they come and go with the season) it is possible to find apparently conflicting High Court authority, which needs to be resolved by the Court of Appeal/House of Lords. Naturally the art of distinguishing a previous **case** is one of the main skills of the advocate.

Procedural law: the rules and principles which govern the way in which a **case** is commenced and managed. Cf, **substantive law.**

Protecting one's position: best done by an offer to settle (**claimant**) or a payment into court (**defendant**).

Public funding: the successor to Legal Aid, enabling **claimants** who have a sufficiently strong case and limited financial means to fund lawyers to act on their behalf. Still available in **clinical negligence actions** but abolished in all other **personal injury actions.**

Punitive interest: see **payment into court** and **offer to settle.**

Quantum: legal shorthand for the value of the **claim.**

Reasonable skill and care: the legal standard which determines whether a **defendant** is in **breach of duty.**

Remedy, remedies: the options available to a Court in determining the **claim.** Usually in an **action** for **personal injuries,** the only available (or useful) **remedy** is **damages.**

Res ipsa loquitur: in Latin, "the thing speaks for itself". A legal principle of evidence which describes a situation where a Court may sometimes infer negligence simply from the fact of an adverse outcome. Of little practical use in **clinical negligence actions**.

Schedule of loss: a document which sets out the financial loss claimed by the claimant. The defendant responds with a Counter-Schedule.

Single joint expert: a special type of expert witness who is instructed (either by agreement or by order of the court) to give his opinion to both parties.

Skeleton argument: a document drafted by an advocate which summarises the (legal and evidential) arguments which he wishes to raise before the judge, designed to save court time.

Solicitor: the lawyer with day-to-day conduct of any case. All solicitors conducting clinical negligence litigation for **defendants** are experienced in the field. Increasingly they will handle all stages of litigation except (possibly) the pleadings and (usually) the trial, only seeking further input from a **barrister** for important tactical or technical queries. **Solicitors** may now qualify to conduct **cases** in court themselves.

Special damages, pecuniary loss, financial loss, past loss, future loss: the element of an award of **damages** which compensates the **claimant** for the financial **loss** which he has suffered in the past and will suffer in the future. Past **loss** is capable of detailed calculation; future **loss** is of necessity slightly more speculative.

Standard of proof: the measure by which a court must be satisfied before it finds in favour of the party who brings the **claim**. In civil (i.e. non-criminal) **cases**, the **standard of proof** is the **balance of probabilities** (i.e. whether something is more likely than not, or over 50%). (Cf criminal **cases**, where the **standard of proof** is beyond reasonable doubt, a much higher degree of certainty). The fact that, to a scientist, there is no proof in support of a certain proposition will not prevent a court from making a determination in favour of the **claimant**. In particular a close temporal association between an operation and an adverse outcome may be of much greater weight in a court **case** than it could be in a clinical trial.

Statement of case: see **pleading**.

Substantive law: the law and principles which govern whether a **claim** will succeed or not.

Sue: to commence legal proceedings.

Summons: see **claim** form.

Supervening cause: a specific **defence**, argued by a **defendant** where a subsequent party becomes involved in the patient's care, and whose **negligence** is said to render the first **defendant**'s own **negligence** irrelevant. Rarely successful in practice.

Time-barred: see **limitation**.

Tort, law of: An area of civil (i.e. non-criminal) law which governs the relationship between people who are not in a **contract**ual relationship. Such people may, despite the absence of a **contract**, owe duties to each other, breach of which may give rise to the right to a remedy. The main sub-category is **negligence**, but other categories include: nuisance; breach of statutory duty; trespass to the person.

Tracks; small-claims track, fast-track, multi-track: each defended **case** will be allocated to one of these tracks, depending on its value and complexity. Different tracks have different rules and provisions for, e.g. **costs**, witnesses, length of trial etc. Most if not all **clinical negligence cases** will be allocated to the **multi-track**, which provides maximum flexibility.

Trial: the Court hearing at which the issues between the parties are determined, when the judge will hear the **evidence** and arguments by the advocates, make his findings of fact, draw inferences from those findings if necessary and determine whether the **claimant** succeeds and, if so, the remedy (and its extent) which is appropriate.

Writ: see **claim form**.

Further information

Useful Web Sites

www.facs.org American College of Surgeons

www.aamc.org Association of American Medical

www.apil.com The Association of Personal Injury Lawyers

www.asgbi.org.uk The Association of Surgeons of Great Britain and Ireland

www.mcb.co.uk/bjcg The British Journal of Clinical Governance

web.bma.org.uk The British Medical Association

www.clinical-disputes-forum.org.uk The Clinical Disputes Forum

www.doh.gov.uk Department of Health

www.doh.gov.uk/humanrights Department of Health - The Human Rights Act 1998

www.doh.gov.uk/mediation Department of Health article 'Mediating medical negligence claims: an option for the future?'

www.doctors.net.uk A service for doctors by doctors

www.echr.coe.int European Court of Human Rights

www.esvs.org The European Society of Vascular Surgery

www.expertpages.com Expert pages - Directory of Expert Witnesses and Consultants

www.ewi.org.uk Expert Witness Institute

www.gmc-uk.org The General Medical Council

www.open.gov.uk CCTA Government Information Service

www.health.ombudsman.org.uk The Health Service Ombudsman

www.hmso.gov.uk Her Majesty's Stationery Office

www.homeoffice.gov.uk The Home Office

www.homeoffice.gov.uk/hract Home Office Human Rights Unit

www.iss.sic.ch International Society of Surgery

www.lawontheweb.co.uk Law on the web - a legal information site

www.lawsociety.org.uk The Law Society

www.lawtel.co.uk Lawtel - the law on line

www.legalservices.gov.uk The Legal Services Commission

www.open.gov.uk/lcd/lcdhome The Lord Chancellor's Department

www.open.gov.uk/lcd/civil/procrules The Lord Chancellor's Department -
Civil Procedure Rules

www.the-mdu.com The Medical Defence Union

www.mddus.com The Medical & Dental Defence Union of Scotland

www.mps.org.uk The Medical Protection Society

www.medico-legalsociety.org.uk The medico-legal society

www.nao.gov.uk The National Audit Office

www.nhs.uk The National Health Service

www.cgsupport.org.uk NHS Clinical Governance Support Team

www.nhsdirect.nhs.uk National Health Service Direct

www.nice.org.uk/nice-web The National Institute for Clinical Excellence

www.rcseng.ac.uk The Royal College of Surgeons

www.roysocmed.ac.uk The Royal Society of Medicine

www.stpaul.co.uk St. Paul International Insurance Company - Medical
professional liability

www.official-documents.co.uk The Stationery Office

www.parliament.the-stationery-office.co.uk United Kingdom Parliament

www.jspubs.com UK Register of Expert Witnesses

www.vssgbi.co.uk The Vascular Surgical Society of Great Britain and Ireland

Appendix I

The GMC guideline

Seeking patients' consent: the ethical considerations

February 1999

Contents

213

Guidance to doctors

Being registered with the General Medical Council gives you rights and privileges. In return, you must meet the standards of competence, care and conduct set by the GMC.

This guideline sets out the principles of good practice which all registered doctors are expected to follow when seeking patients' informed consent to investigations, treatment, screening or research. It enlarges on the general principles set out in paragraph 12 of the booklet 'Good Medical Practice.'

Introduction

1. Successful relationships between doctors and patients depend on trust. To establish that trust you must respect patients' autonomy - their right to decide whether or not to undergo any medical intervention even where a refusal may result in harm to themselves or in their own death[1]. Patients must be given sufficient information, in a way that they can understand, to enable them to exercise their right to make informed decisions about their care.

2. This right is protected in law, and you are expected to be aware of the legal principles set by relevant case law in this area[2]. Existing case law gives a guide to what can be considered minimum requirements of good practice in seeking informed consent from patients.

3. Effective communication is the key to enabling patients to make informed decisions. You must take appropriate steps to find out what patients want to know and ought to know about their condition and its treatment. Open, helpful dialogue of this kind with patients leads to clarity of objectives and understanding, and strengthens the quality of the doctor/patient relationship. It provides an agreed framework within which the doctor can respond effectively to the individual needs of the patient. Additionally, patients who have been able to make properly informed decisions are more likely to cooperate fully with the agreed management of their conditions.

Consent to investigation and treatment

Providing sufficient information

4. Patients have a right to information about their condition and the treatment options available to them. The amount of information you give each patient will vary, according to factors such as the nature of the condition, the complexity of the treatment, the risks associated with the treatment or procedure, and the patient's own wishes. For example, patients may need more information to make an informed decision about a procedure which carries a high risk of failure or adverse side effects; or about an investigation for a condition which, if present, could have serious implications for the patient's employment, social or personal life[3].

214

5. The information which patients want or ought to know, before deciding whether to consent to treatment or an investigation, may include:

- details of the diagnosis, and prognosis, and the likely prognosis if the condition is left untreated;
- uncertainties about the diagnosis including options for further investigation prior to treatment;
- options for treatment or management of the condition, including the option not to treat;
- the purpose of a proposed investigation or treatment; details of the procedures or therapies involved, including subsidiary treatment such as methods of pain relief; how the patient should prepare for the procedure; and details of what the patient might experience during or after the procedure including common and serious side effects;
- for each option, explanations of the likely benefits and the probabilities of success; and discussion of any serious or frequently occurring risks, and of any lifestyle changes which may be caused by, or necessitated by, the treatment;
- advice about whether a proposed treatment is experimental;
- how and when the patient's condition and any side effects will be monitored or re-assessed;
- the name of the doctor who will have overall responsibility for the treatment and, where appropriate, names of the senior members of his or her team;
- whether doctors in training will be involved, and the extent to which students may be involved in an investigation or treatment;
- a reminder that patients can change their minds about a decision at any time;
- a reminder that patients have a right to seek a second opinion;
- where applicable, details of costs or charges which the patient may have to meet.

6. When providing information you must do your best to find out about patients' individual needs and priorities. For example, patients' beliefs, culture, occupation or other factors may have a bearing on the information they need in order to reach a decision. You should not make assumptions about patients' views, but discuss these matters with them, and ask them whether they have any concerns about the treatment or the risks it may involve. You should provide patients with appropriate information, which should include an explanation of any risks to which they may attach particular significance. Ask patients whether they have understood the information and whether they would like more before making a decision.

7. You must not exceed the scope of the authority given by a patient, except in an emergency[4]. Therefore, if you are the doctor providing treatment or undertaking an investigation, you must give the patient a clear explanation of the scope of consent being sought. This will apply particularly where:

- treatment will be provided in stages with the possibility of later adjustments;
- different doctors (or other health care workers) provide particular elements of an investigation or treatment (for example anaesthesia in surgery);
- a number of different investigations or treatments are involved;
- uncertainty about the diagnosis, or about the appropriate range of options for treatment, may be resolved only in the light of findings once investigation or treatment is underway, and when the patient may be unable to participate in decision making.

In such cases, you should explain how decisions would be made about whether or when to move from one stage or one form of treatment to another. There should be a clear agreement about whether the patient consents to all or only parts of the proposed plan of investigation or treatment, and whether further consent will have to be sought at a later stage.

8. You should raise with patients the possibility of additional problems coming to light during a procedure when the patient is unconscious or otherwise unable to make a decision. You should seek consent to treat any problems which you think may arise and ascertain whether there are any procedures to which the patient would object, or prefer to give further thought to before you proceed. You must abide by patients' decisions on these issues. If in exceptional circumstances you decide, while the patient is unconscious, to treat a condition which falls outside the scope of the patient's consent, your decision may be challenged in the courts, or be the subject of a complaint to your employing authority or the GMC. You should therefore seek the views of an experienced colleague, wherever possible, before providing the treatment. And you must be prepared to explain and justify your decision. You must tell the patient what you have done and why, as soon as the patient is sufficiently recovered to understand.

Responding to questions

9. You must respond honestly to any questions the patient raises and, as far as possible, answer as fully as the patient wishes. In some cases, a patient may ask about other treatments that are unproven or ineffective. Some patients may want to know whether any of the risks or benefits of treatment are affected by the choice of institution or doctor providing the care. You must answer such questions as fully, accurately and objectively as possible.

Withholding information

10. You should not withhold information necessary for decision making unless you judge that disclosure of some relevant information would cause the patient serious harm. In this context serious harm does not mean the patient would become upset, or decide to refuse treatment.

11. No-one may make decisions on behalf of a competent adult. If patients ask you to withhold information and make decisions on their behalf, or nominate a relative or third party to make decisions for them, you should explain the importance of them knowing the options open to them, and what the treatment they may receive will involve. If they insist they do not want to know in detail about their condition and its treatment, you should still provide basic information about the treatment. If a relative asks you to withhold information, you must seek the views of the patient. Again, you should not withhold relevant information unless you judge that this would cause the patient serious harm.

12. In any case where you withhold relevant information from the patient you must record this, and the reason for doing so, in the patient's medical records and you must be prepared to explain and justify your decision.

Presenting information to patients

13. Obtaining informed consent cannot be an isolated event. It involves a continuing dialogue between you and your patients which keeps them abreast of changes in their condition and the treatment or investigation you propose. Whenever possible, you should discuss treatment options at a time when the patient is best able to understand and retain the information. To be sure that your patient understands, you should give clear explanations and give the patient time to ask questions. In particular, you should:

- use up to date written material, visual and other aids to explain complex aspects of the investigation, diagnosis or treatment where appropriate and/or practicable;
- make arrangements, wherever possible, to meet particular language and communication needs, for example through translations, independent interpreters, signers, or the patient's representative;
- where appropriate, discuss with patients the possibility of bringing a relative or friend, or making a tape recording of the consultation;
- explain the probabilities of success, or the risk of failure of, or harm associated with options for treatment, using accurate data;
- ensure that information which patients may find distressing is given to them in a considerate way. Provide patients with information about counselling services and patient support groups, where appropriate;
- allow patients sufficient time to reflect, before and after making a decision, especially where the information is complex or the severity of the risks is great. Where patients have difficulty understanding information, or there is a lot of information to absorb, it may be appropriate to provide it in manageable amounts, with appropriate written or other back-up material, over a period of time, or to repeat it;
- involve nursing or other members of the health care team in discussions with the patient, where appropriate. They may have valuable knowledge of the patient's background or particular concerns, for example in identifying what risks the patient should be told about;
- ensure that, where treatment is not to start until some time after consent has been obtained, the patient is given a clear route for reviewing their decision with the person providing the treatment.

Who obtains consent

14. If you are the doctor providing treatment or undertaking an investigation, it is your responsibility to discuss it with the patient and obtain consent, as you will have a comprehensive understanding of the procedure or treatment, how it is carried out, and the risks attached to it. Where this is not practicable, you may delegate these tasks provided you ensure that the person to whom you delegate:

- is suitably trained and qualified;
- has sufficient knowledge of the proposed investigation or treatment, and understands the risks involved;
- acts in accordance with the guidance in this booklet.

You will remain responsible for ensuring that, before you start any treatment, the patient has been given sufficient time and information to make an informed decision, and has given consent to the procedure or investigation.

Ensuring voluntary decision making

15. It is for the patient, not the doctor, to determine what is in the patient's own best interests. Nonetheless, you may wish to recommend a treatment or a course of action to patients, but you must not put pressure on patients to accept your advice. In discussions with patients, you should:

217

❖ give a balanced view of the options;
❖ explain the need for informed consent.

You must declare any potential conflicts of interest, for example where you or your organisation benefit financially from use of a particular drug or treatment, or treatment at a particular institution.

16. Pressure may be put on patients by employers, insurance companies or others to undergo particular tests or accept treatment. You should do your best to ensure that patients have considered the options and reached their own decision. You should take appropriate action if you believe patients are being offered inappropriate or unlawful financial or other rewards.

17. Patients who are detained by the police or immigration services, or are in prison, and those detained under the provisions of any mental health legislation may be particularly vulnerable. Where such patients have a right to decline treatment you should do your best to ensure that they know this, and are able to exercise this right.

Emergencies

18. In an emergency, where consent cannot be obtained, you may provide medical treatment to anyone who needs it, provided the treatment is limited to what is immediately necessary to save life or avoid significant deterioration in the patient's health. However, you must still respect the terms of any valid advance refusal which you know about, or is drawn to your attention. You should tell the patient what has been done, and why, as soon as the patient is sufficiently recovered to understand.

Establishing capacity to make decisions

19. You must work on the presumption that every adult has the capacity to decide whether to consent to, or refuse, proposed medical intervention, unless it is shown that they cannot understand information presented in a clear way[5]. If a patient's choice appears irrational, or does not accord with your view of what is in the patient's best interests, that is not evidence in itself that the patient lacks competence. In such circumstances it may be appropriate to review with the patient whether all reasonable steps have been taken to identify and meet their information needs (see paragraphs 5-17). Where you need to assess a patient's capacity to make a decision, you should consult the guidance issued by professional bodies[6].

Fluctuating capacity
20. Where patients have difficulty retaining information, or are only intermittently competent to make a decision, you should provide any assistance they might need to reach an informed decision. You should record any decision made while the patients were competent, including the key elements of the consultation. You should review any decision made whilst they were competent, at appropriate intervals before treatment starts, to establish that their views are consistently held and can be relied on.

Mentally incapacitated patients

21. No-one can give or withhold consent to treatment on behalf of a mentally incapacitated patient[7.] You must first assess the patient's capacity to make an informed decision about the treatment. If patients lack capacity to decide, provided they comply, you may carry out an investigation or treatment, which may include treatment for any mental disorder[8], that you judge to be in their best interests. However, if they do not comply, you may compulsorily treat them for any mental disorder only within the safeguards laid down by the Mental Health Act 1983[9], and any physical disorder arising from that mental disorder, in line with the guidance in the Code of Practice of the Mental Health Commission[10]. You should seek the courts' approval for any non-therapeutic or controversial treatments which are not directed at their mental disorder.

Advance statements

22. If you are treating a patient who has lost capacity to consent to or refuse treatment, for example through onset or progress of a mental disorder or other disability, you should try to find out whether the patient has previously indicated preferences in an advance statement ('advance directives' or 'living wills'). You must respect any refusal of treatment given when the patient was competent, provided the decision in the advance statement is clearly applicable to the present circumstances, and there is no reason to believe that the patient has changed his/her mind. Where an advance statement of this kind is not available, the patient's known wishes should be taken into account - see paragraph 25 on the 'best interests' principle.

Children

23. You must assess a child's capacity to decide whether to consent to or refuse proposed investigation or treatment before you provide it. In general, a competent child will be able to understand the nature, purpose and possible consequences of the proposed investigation or treatment, as well as the consequences of non-treatment. Your assessment must take account of the relevant laws or legal precedents in this area[11]. You should bear in mind that:

- ❖ at age 16 a young person can be treated as an adult and can be presumed to have capacity to decide;
- ❖ under age 16 children may have capacity to decide, depending on their ability to understand what is involved[12];
- ❖ where a competent child refuses treatment, a person with parental responsibility or the court may authorise investigation or treatment which is in the child's best interests. The position is different in Scotland, where those with parental responsibility cannot authorise procedures a competent child has refused. Legal advice may be helpful on how to deal with such cases.

24. Where a child under 16 years old is not competent to give or withhold their informed consent, a person with parental responsibility may authorise investigations or treatment which are in the child's best interests[13]. This person may also refuse any intervention, where they consider that refusal to be in the child's best interests, but you are not bound by such a refusal and may seek a ruling from the court. In an emergency where you consider that it is in the child's best interests to proceed, you may treat the child, provided it is limited to that treatment which is reasonably required in that emergency.

219

'Best interests' principle

25. In deciding what options may be reasonably considered as being in the best interests of a patient who lacks capacity to decide, you should take into account:

❖ options for treatment or investigation which are clinically indicated;
❖ any evidence of the patient's previously expressed preferences, including an advance statement;
❖ your own and the health care team's knowledge of the patient's background, such as cultural, religious, or employment considerations;
❖ views about the patient's preferences given by a third party who may have other knowledge of the patient, for example the patient's partner, family, carer, tutor-dative (Scotland), or a person with parental responsibility;
❖ which option least restricts the patient's future choices, where more than one option (including non-treatment) seems reasonable in the patient's best interest.

Applying to the court

26. Where a patient's capacity to consent is in doubt, or where differences of opinion about his or her best interests cannot be resolved satisfactorily, you should consult more experienced colleagues and, where appropriate, seek legal advice on whether it is necessary to apply to the court for a ruling. You should seek the court's approval where a patient lacks capacity to consent to a medical intervention which is non-therapeutic or controversial, for example contraceptive sterilisation, organ donation, withdrawal of life support from a patient in a persistent vegetative state. Where you decide to apply to a court you should, as soon as possible, inform the patient and his or her representative of your decision and of his or her right to be represented at the hearing.

Forms of consent

27. To determine whether patients have given informed consent to any proposed investigation or treatment, you must consider how well they have understood the details and implications of what is proposed, and not simply the form in which their consent has been expressed or recorded.

Express consent
28. Patients can indicate their informed consent either orally or in writing. In some cases, the nature of the risks to which the patient might be exposed make it important that a written record is available of the patient's consent and other wishes in relation to the proposed investigation and treatment. This helps to ensure later understanding between you, the patient, and anyone else involved in carrying out the procedure or providing care. Except in an emergency, where the patient has capacity to give consent you should obtain written consent in cases where:

❖ the treatment or procedure is complex, or involves significant risks and/or side effects;
❖ providing clinical care is not the primary purpose of the investigation or examination;
❖ there may be significant consequences for the patient's employment, social or personal life;
❖ the treatment is part of a research programme.

29. You must use the patient's case notes and/or a consent form to detail the key elements of the discussion with the patient, including the nature of information provided, specific requests by the patient, details of the scope of the consent given.

Statutory requirements

30. Some statutes require written consent to be obtained for particular treatments (for example some fertility treatments). You must follow the law in these areas.

Implied consent

31. You should be careful about relying on a patient's apparent compliance with a procedure as a form of consent. For example, the fact that a patient lies down on an examination couch does not in itself indicate that the patient has understood what you propose to do and why.

Reviewing consent

32. A signed consent form is not sufficient evidence that a patient has given, or still gives, informed consent to the proposed treatment in all its aspects. You, or a member of the team, must review the patient's decision close to the time of treatment, and especially where:

❖ significant time has elapsed between obtaining consent and the start of treatment;

❖ there have been material changes in the patient's condition, or in any aspects of the proposed treatment plan, which might invalidate the patient's existing consent;

❖ new, potentially relevant information has become available, for example about the risks of the treatment, or about other treatment options.

Consent to screening

33. Screening (which may involve testing) healthy or asymptomatic people to detect genetic predispositions or early signs of debilitating or life threatening conditions can be an important tool in providing effective care. But the uncertainties involved in screening may be great, for example the risk of false positive or false negative results. Some findings may potentially have serious medical, social or financial consequences not only for the individuals, but for their relatives. In some cases the fact of having been screened may itself have serious implications.

34. You must ensure that anyone considering whether to consent to screening can make a properly informed decision. As far as possible, you should ensure that screening would not be contrary to the individual's interest. You must pay particular attention to ensuring that the information the person wants or ought to have is identified and provided. You should be careful to explain clearly:

❖ the purpose of the screening;

❖ the likelihood of positive/negative findings and possibility of false positive/negative results;

221

- ❖   the uncertainties and risks attached to the screening process;
- ❖   any significant medical, social or financial implications of screening for the particular condition or predisposition;
- ❖   follow up plans, including availability of counselling and support services.

If you are considering the possibility of screening children, or adults who are not able to decide for themselves, you should refer to the guidance at paragraphs 19-25. In appropriate cases, you should take account of the guidance issued by bodies such as the Advisory Committee on Genetic Testing [14].

Consent to research

35. Research involving clinical trials of drugs or treatments, and research into the causes of, or possible treatment for, a particular condition, is important in increasing doctors' ability to provide effective care for present and future patients. The benefits of the research may, however, be uncertain and may not be experienced by the person participating in the research. In addition, the risk involved for research participants may be difficult to identify or to assess in advance. If you carry out or participate in research involving patients or volunteers, it is particularly important that you ensure:

- ❖   as far as you are able, that the research is not contrary to the individual's interests;
- ❖   that participants understand that it is research and that the results are not predictable.

36. You must take particular care to be sure that anyone you ask to consider taking part in research is given the fullest possible information, presented in terms and a form that they can understand. This must include any information about possible benefits and risks; evidence that a research ethics committee has given approval; and advice that they can withdraw at any time. You should ensure that participants have the opportunity to read and consider the research information leaflet. You must allow them sufficient time to reflect on the implications of participating in the study. You must not put pressure on anyone to take part in research. You must obtain the person's consent in writing. Before starting any research you must always obtain approval from a properly constituted research ethics committee.

37. You should seek further advice where your research will involve adults who are not able to make decisions for themselves, or children. You should be aware that in these cases the legal position is complex or unclear, and there is currently no general consensus on how to balance the possible risks and benefits to such vulnerable individuals against the public interest in conducting research. (A number of public consultation exercises are under way.) You should consult the guidance issued by bodies such as the Medical Research Council and the medical royal colleges [16] to keep up to date. You should also seek advice from the relevant research ethics committee where appropriate.

Notes

1 This right to decide applies equally to pregnant women as to other patients, and includes the right to refuse treatment where the treatment is intended to benefit the unborn child. See St George's Healthcare NHS Trust v S [1998] Fam Law 526 and 662, and MB (an adult: medical treatment) [1997] 2 FCR 541,CA.

2 Advice can be obtained from medical defence bodies such as the Medical Defence Union, Medical Protection Society, the Medical and Dental Defence Union of Scotland, or professional associations such as the BMA, or your employing organisation.

3 Our booklet 'Serious Communicable Diseases' gives specific guidance on seeking consent to testing for conditions like HIV, Hepatitis B and C.

4 Guidance on treating patients in emergencies is included in paragraph 18.

5 A patient will be competent if he or she can: comprehend information, it having been presented to them in a clear way; believe it; and retain it long enough to weigh it up and make a decision. From Re C (Adult: Refusal of Medical Treatment) [1994] 1 All ER 819. But seek legal advice, in case of doubt.

6 For example the BMA/Law Society publication, 'Assessment of Mental Capacity: Guidance for Doctors and Lawyers' available from the BMA.

7 Except in Scotland where a 'tutor-dative' with appropriate authority may make medical decisions on behalf of the patient. Seek legal advice, in case of doubt.

8 Legal advice should be obtained in case of doubt. A relevant precedent is the case of Regina v Bournewood Community and Mental Health NHS Trust ex parte L [1998] 3 All ER, 289 HL.

9 And similar legislation in Scotland and Northern Ireland.

10 Code of Practice Dec 1998 pursuant to s118 of the Mental Health Act 1983.

11 You should consult your medical defence body or professional association for up to date advice. Appendix A lists some of the relevant key legislation.

12 Age of Legal Capacity (Scotland) Act 1991 (Section 2.4); Gillick v West Norfolk and Wisbech AHA ALL ER [1985], 3 ALL ER 402.

13 This also applies to young people between 16 and 18 years old, except in Scotland.

14 ACGT can be contacted at: ACGT Secretariat, Department of Health, Room 401, Wellington House, 133-135 Waterloo Road, London, SE1 8UG. Telephone: 020 7972 4017.

15 Consult your medical defence body, a professional association such as the BMA, or your employing organisation.

16 Appendix B gives an indicative list of published guidance. The GMC plans to publish further guidance on research.

APPENDIX A

Children and Consent to Treatment and Testing: Some Key Legislation

England & Wales

❖ Family Law Reform Act 1969.
❖ Gillick v West Norfolk and Wisbech AHA [1985], 3 AER 402.
❖ Children Act 1989.

Scotland

❖ Age of Legal Capacity (Scotland) Act 1991.
❖ Children Act (Scotland) 1995, Section 6, Part 1.

Northern Ireland

❖ Age of Majority Act 1969, Section 4.

APPENDIX B

Other Guidance on Research: Indicative List of Relevant Publications

'Good Medical Practice', paragraphs 55-56. The General Medical Council, 178-202 Great Portland Street, London, W1N 6JE. 1998.

'The Ethical Conduct of Research on Children'. MRC Ethics Series. The Medical Research Council, 20 Park Crescent, London, W1N 4AL. 1991 and 1993.

'Responsibility in Investigations on Human Participants and Materials and on Personal Information'. MRC Ethics Series. The Medical Research Council. 1992.

'The Ethical Conduct of Research on the Mentally Incapacitated'. MRC Ethics series. The Medical Research Council. 1991 and 1993.

'Research Involving Patients'. The Royal College of Physicians of London, 11 St Andrew's Place, London, NW1 4LE. January 1990.

'Guidelines on the Practice of Ethics Committees in Medical Research Involving Human Subjects'. Second Edition. The Royal College of Physicians of London, 11 St Andrew's Place, London, NW1 4LE. January 1990.

'Local Research Ethics Committees' (HSG(91)5). Department of Health, Richmond House, 79 Whitehall, London, SW1A 2NS. 1991.

'Multi Centre Research Committees' (HSG(97)23). Department of Health, Richmond House, 79 Whitehall, London SW1A 2NS. 1997.

'ABPI Guidance Note. Patient Information and Consents for Clinical Trials'. Association of British Pharmaceutical Industry, 12 Whitehall, London, SW1A 2DY. May 1997.

'International Ethical Guidelines for Biomedical Research Involving Human Subjects'. Council for International Organisations of Medical Sciences (CIOMS), c/o World Health Organisation, Avenue Appia, 1211 Geneva 27, Switzerland.

'Charter for Ethical Research in Maternity Care.' 1997. National Childbirth Trust, Alexandra House, Oldham Terrace, Acton, London W3 6NH.

'Human Tissue: Ethical and Legal Issues' Nuffield Council on Bioethics, 28 Bedford Square, London WC1B 3EG April 1995.

Reproduced with the kind permission of the General Medical Council, 178 Great Portland Street, London, W1N 6JE.

Appendix II

Civil Procedure Rules 1999 Part 35

EXPERTS AND ASSESSORS

CONTENTS OF THIS PART

225

DUTY TO RESTRICT EXPERT EVIDENCE

35.1   Expert evidence shall be restricted to that which is reasonably required to resolve the proceedings.

INTERPRETATION

35.2   A reference to an 'expert' in this Part is a reference to an expert who has been instructed to give or prepare evidence for the purpose of court proceedings.

EXPERTS - OVERRIDING DUTY TO THE COURT

35.3   (1) It is the duty of an expert to help the court on the matters within his expertise.

(2) This duty overrides any obligation to the person from whom he has received instructions or by whom he is paid.

COURT'S POWER TO RESTRICT EXPERT EVIDENCE

35.4   (1) No party may call an expert or put in evidence an expert's report without the court's permission.

(2) When a party applies for permission under this rule he must identify -

    (a) the field in which he wishes to rely on expert evidence; and

    (b) where practicable the expert in that field on whose evidence he wishes to rely.

(3) If permission is granted under this rule it shall be in relation only to the expert named or the field identified under paragraph (2).

(4) The court may limit the amount of the expert's fees and expenses that the party who wishes to rely on the expert may recover from any other party.

GENERAL REQUIREMENT FOR EXPERT EVIDENCE TO BE GIVEN IN A WRITTEN REPORT

35.5   (1) Expert evidence is to be given in a written report unless the court directs otherwise.

(2) If a claim is on the fast track, the court will not direct an expert to attend a hearing unless it is necessary to do so in the interests of justice.

WRITTEN QUESTIONS TO EXPERTS

35.6 (1) A party may put to -

(a) an expert instructed by another party; or

(b) a single joint expert appointed under rule 35.7, written questions about his report.

(2) Written questions under paragraph (1) -

(a) may be put once only;

(b) must be put within 28 days of service of the expert's report; and

(c) must be for the purpose only of clarification of the report, unless in any case -

(i) the court gives permission; or

(ii) the other party agrees.

(3) An expert's answers to questions put in accordance with paragraph (1) shall be treated as part of the expert's report.

(4) Where -

(a) a party has put a written question to an expert instructed by another party in accordance with this rule; and

(b) the expert does not answer that question,

the court may make one or both of the following orders in relation to the party who instructed the expert -

(i) that the party may not rely on the evidence of that expert; or

(ii) that the party may not recover the fees and expenses of that expert from any other party.

COURT'S POWER TO DIRECT THAT EVIDENCE IS TO BE GIVEN BY A SINGLE JOINT EXPERT

35.7 (1) Where two or more parties wish to submit expert evidence on a particular issue, the court may direct that the evidence on that issue is to be given by one expert only.

(2) The parties wishing to submit the expert evidence are called 'the instructing parties'.

(3) Where the instructing parties cannot agree who should be the expert, the court may -

(a) select the expert from a list prepared or identified by the instructing parties; or

(b) direct that the expert be selected in such other manner as the court may direct.

INSTRUCTIONS TO A SINGLE JOINT EXPERT

35.8 (1) Where the court gives a direction under rule 35.7 for a single joint expert to be used, each instructing party may give instructions to the expert.

(2) When an instructing party gives instructions to the expert he must, at the same time, send a copy of the instructions to the other instructing parties.

(3) The court may give directions about -

    (a) the payment of the expert's fees and expenses; and

    (b) any inspection, examination or experiments which the expert wishes to carry out.

(4) The court may, before an expert is instructed -

    (a) limit the amount that can be paid by way of fees and expenses to the expert; and

    (b) direct that the instructing parties pay that amount into court.

(5) Unless the court otherwise directs, the instructing parties are jointly and severally liable GL for the payment of the expert's fees and expenses.

POWER OF COURT TO DIRECT A PARTY TO PROVIDE INFORMATION

35.9 Where a party has access to information which is not reasonably available to the other party, the court may direct the party who has access to the information to -

    (a) prepare and file a document recording the information; and

    (b) serve a copy of that document on the other party.

CONTENTS OF REPORT

35.10 (1) An expert's report must comply with the requirements set out in the relevant practice direction.

(2) At the end of an expert's report there must be a statement that -

    (a) the expert understands his duty to the court; and

    (b) he has complied with that duty.

(3) The expert's report must state the substance of all material instructions, whether written or oral, on the basis of which the report was written.

(4) The instructions referred to in paragraph (3) shall not be privileged GL against disclosure but the court will not, in relation to those instructions -

    (a) order disclosure of any specific document; or

    (b) permit any questioning in court, other than by the party who instructed the expert, unless it is satisfied that there are reasonable grounds to consider the statement of instructions given under paragraph (3) to be inaccurate or incomplete.

USE BY ONE PARTY OF EXPERT'S REPORT DISCLOSED BY ANOTHER

35.11 Where a party has disclosed an expert's report, any party may use that expert's report as evidence at the trial.

DISCUSSIONS BETWEEN EXPERTS

35.12 (1) The court may, at any stage, direct a discussion between experts for the purpose of requiring the experts to -

(a) identify the issues in the proceedings; and

(b) where possible, reach agreement on an issue.

(2) The court may specify the issues which the experts must discuss.

(3) The court may direct that following a discussion between the experts they must prepare a statement for the court showing -

(a) those issues on which they agree; and

(b) those issues on which they disagree and a summary of their reasons for disagreeing.

(4) The content of the discussion between the experts shall not be referred to at the trial unless the parties agree.

(5) Where experts reach agreement on an issue during their discussions, the agreement shall not bind the parties unless the parties expressly agree to be bound by the agreement.

CONSEQUENCE OF FAILURE TO DISCLOSE EXPERT'S REPORT

35.13 A party who fails to disclose an expert's report may not use the report at the trial or call the expert to give evidence orally unless the court gives permission.

EXPERT'S RIGHT TO ASK COURT FOR DIRECTIONS

35.14 (1) An expert may file a written request for directions to assist him in carrying out his function as an expert.

(2) An expert may request directions under paragraph (1) without giving notice to any party.

(3) The court, when it gives directions, may also direct that a party be served with -

(a) a copy of the directions; and

(b) a copy of the request for directions.

ASSESSORS

35.15 (1) This rule applies where the court appoints one or more persons (an 'assessor') under section 70 of the Supreme Court Act 1981[41] or section 63 of the County Courts Act 1984[42].

(2) The assessor shall assist the court in dealing with a matter in which the assessor has skill and experience.

(3) An assessor shall take such part in the proceedings as the court may direct and in particular the court may -

(a) direct the assessor to prepare a report for the court on any matter at issue in the proceedings; and

(b) direct the assessor to attend the whole or any part of the trial to advise the court on any such matter.

(4) If the assessor prepares a report for the court before the trial has begun -

(a) the court will send a copy to each of the parties; and

(b) the parties may use it at trial.

(5) The remuneration to be paid to the assessor for his services shall be determined by the court and shall form part of the costs of the proceedings.

(6) The court may order any party to deposit in the court office a specified sum in respect of the assessor's fees and, where it does so, the assessor will not be asked to act until the sum has been deposited.

(7) Paragraphs (5) and (6) do not apply where the remuneration of the assessor is to be paid out of money provided by Parliament.

41 1981 c.54.
42 1984 c.28. Section 63 was amended by S.I. 1998/2940.

Source:-
Civil Procedure Rules - January 1999
The Lord Chancellor's Department
Selborne House
54-60 Victoria Street
London
SW1E 6QW

PRACTICE DIRECTION - EXPERTS AND ASSESSORS

THIS PRACTICE DIRECTION SUPPLEMENTS CPR PART 35

Part 35 is intended to limit the use of oral expert evidence to that which is reasonably required. In addition, where possible, matters requiring expert evidence should be dealt with by a single expert. Permission of the court is always required either to call an expert or to put an expert's report in evidence.

FORM AND CONTENT OF EXPERT'S REPORTS

1.1 An expert's report should be addressed to the court and not to the party from whom the expert has received his instructions.

1.2 An expert's report must:

(1) give details of the expert's qualifications,

(2) give details of any literature or other material which the expert has relied on in making the report,

(3) say who carried out any test or experiment which the expert has used for the report and whether or not the test or experiment has been carried out under the expert's supervision,

(4) give the qualifications of the person who carried out any such test or experiment, and

(5) where there is a range of opinion on the matters dealt with in the report -

(i) summarise the range of opinion, and

(ii) give reasons for his own opinion,

(6) contain a summary of the conclusions reached,

(7) contain a statement that the expert understands his duty to the court and has complied with that duty (rule 35.10(2)), and

(8) contain a statement setting out the substance of all material instructions (whether written or oral). The statement should summarise the facts and instructions given to the expert which are material to the opinions expressed in the report or upon which those opinions are based (rule 35.10(3)).

1.3 An expert's report must be verified by a statement of truth as well as containing the statements required in paragraph 1.2 (7) and (8) above.

1.4 The form of the statement of truth is as follows: 'I believe that the facts I have stated in this report are true and that the opinions I have expressed are correct.'

1.5 Attention is drawn to rule 32.14 which sets out the consequences of verifying a document containing a false statement without an honest belief in its truth.

(For information about statements of truth see Part 22 and the practice direction which supplements it.)

1.6   In addition, an expert's report should comply with the requirements of any approved expert's protocol.

INFORMATION

2   Under Part 35.9 the court may direct a party with access to information which is not reasonably available to another party to serve on that other party a document which records the information. The document served must include sufficient details of all the facts, tests, experiments and assumptions which underlie any part of the information to enable the party on whom it is served to make, or to obtain, a proper interpretation of the information and an assessment of its significance.

INSTRUCTIONS

3   The instructions referred to in paragraph 1.2(8) will not be protected by privilege (see rule 35.10(4)). But cross-examination of the expert on the contents of his instructions will not be allowed unless the court permits it (or unless the party who gave the instructions consents to it). Before it gives permission the court must be satisfied that there are reasonable grounds to consider that the statement in the report of the substance of the instructions is inaccurate or incomplete. If the court is so satisfied, it will allow the cross-examination where it appears to be in the interests of justice to do so.

QUESTIONS TO EXPERTS

4.1   Questions asked for the purpose of clarifying the expert's report (see rule 35.6) should be put, in writing, to the expert not later than 28 days after receipt of the expert's report (see paragraphs 1.2 to 1.5 above as to verification).

4.2   Where a party sends a written question or questions direct to an expert and the other party is represented by solicitors, a copy of the questions should, at the same time, be sent to those solicitors.

4.3   The party or parties instructing the expert must pay any fees charged by that expert for answering questions put under rule 35.6. This does not affect any decision of the court as to the party who is ultimately to bear the expert's costs.

SINGLE EXPERT

5   Where the court has directed that the evidence on a particular issue is
     to be given by one expert only (rule 35.7) but there are a number of
     disciplines relevant to that issue, a leading expert in the dominant
     discipline should be identified as the single expert. He should prepare
     the general part of the report and be responsible for annexing or
     incorporating the contents of any reports from experts in other
     disciplines.

ASSESSORS

6.1 An assessor may be appointed to assist the court under rule 35.15. Not
     less than 21 days before making any such appointment, the court will
     notify each party in writing of the name of the proposed assessor, of the
     matter in respect of which the assistance of the assessor will be sought
     and of the qualifications of the assessor to give that assistance.
6.2 Where any person has been proposed for appointment as an assessor,
     objection to him, either personally or in respect of his qualification, may
     be taken by any party.
6.3 Any such objection must be made in writing and filed with the court
     within 7 days of receipt of the notification referred to in paragraph 6.1
     and will be taken into account by the court in deciding whether or not to
     make the appointment (section 63(5) of the County Courts Act 1984).
6.4 Copies of any report prepared by the assessor will be sent to each of
     the parties but the assessor will not give oral evidence or be open to
     cross-examination or questioning.

Source:-
Civil Procedure Rules - August 1999
The Lord Chancellor's Department
Selborne House
54-60 Victoria Street
London
SW1E 6QW

Crown copyright material is reproduced with the permission of the Controller of
Her Majesty's Stationery Office.

233

APPENDIX II

234

Appendix III

Draft structure

of a

medical report

Please note that this is just an example of a medical report for guidance. There are many different styles of reports, which may need to vary according to the subject of the report.

Medical Report prepared on

Claimant's Name:

Claimant's Address:

Date of Birth:

Date of Accident:

Time off Work:

Occupation:

This report prepared by:

Type of specialist:

Qualifications/Title:

Disclosure of interest:

Date of examination:

Examination venue:

Date of report:

Report requested by:

Reference:

Documents available for preparation of report include:

       e.g.   1. Hospital Records
                 2. GP Notes
                 3. Xrays
                 4. Other relevant documents

Contents

1. Instructions

1.01 Mandate

I have been asked by _____ to provide a medical report on _____ following an accident on _____.

2. Enquiry

2.01 Mechanism of accident
2.02 Mechanism of injury
2.03 Injuries sustained
      List all injuries, both immediate and delayed
2.04 Treatment
         a) Immediate
         b) Subsequent
2.05 Claimant's Comments
2.06 Progress of symptoms
      If necessary use sub headings from 2.03 of the injuries sustained
2.07 Employment
2.08 Social and Domestic
         Hobbies, sports, social life
2.09 Psychological
2.10 Past Medical History
2.11 Review of records
         Hospital records, General Practitioner's notes, etc.
2.12 Present state
         Record all on-going symptoms from list 2.03

3. Examination

Give full details of your examination of any area injured, even if the patient has fully recovered. It is important to document negative findings as well as positive ones.

4. Summary, Opinion and Prognosis

This should include:

❖ the diagnosis of all injuries caused by the accident, causation, how the accident caused each problem, the present situation and current level of disability;

237

❖ future treatment, a recommendation of investigations which could be helpful to the patient;

❖ life expectancy;

❖ effect on future employment and long term health, including estimated time to full recovery and prognosis expressed in time frame with or without treatment.

5. Declaration of Truth

It is important to comply with Lord Woolf's Civil Procedure Rules and a declaration of truth, similar to this one, must be included on all reports.

> "I understand that my duty in writing this report is to help the Court on the matters within my expertise. I understand that this duty overrides any obligation to the person from whom I have received instructions or by whom I am paid.
>
> I confirm that I have complied with that duty in writing my report.
>
> I believe that the facts I have stated in this report are true and that the opinions I have expressed are correct."

Appendix 1.   Curriculum Vitae

This should include qualifications, brief history of career, list of appointments within recent history and any other relevant details.

Appendix 2.   Glossary

Any medical terms which a lay person would not understand can be explained here.

Appendix 3.   References

Appendix 4.   Illustrations

e.g. Diagrams, photographs, etc.

The report must be signed

238

Appendix IV

Guidelines on Experts' Discussions in the Context of Clinical Disputes

In November 1999 the Clinical Disputes Forum published draft guidelines on Experts' Discussions in the Context of Clinical Disputes[1]. The consultation period was extended until mid January 2000. Nine organisations and 19 individuals responded and the working party met again in late February to consider the responses. Much of the greatest controversy was generated by the suggestion in the original draft that experts should conduct their discussions alone. We have now modified that advice and accompanying this revised draft is an explanatory note by Adrian Whitfield QC, a member of the working party. The revisions were discussed by the full Forum at its April meeting.

The Guidelines should be seen in the context of Part 35 of the Civil Procedure Rules and its associated Practice Direction. We have attempted to suggest Guidelines which could usefully be incorporated into the Clinical Negligence Practice Direction (as yet unpublished). The Guidelines should also be seen in the context of the Code of Guidance for Experts previously published in draft form and currently awaiting ratification[2], and in particular with paragraphs 19-22 of the Code.

References

1. Consultation on Guidelines on Experts' Discussions in the Context of Clinical Disputes. (1999) *Clinical Risk* 5(6): 205-208
2. Blom-Cooper L (1999) Draft Code of Guidance for Experts: for Consultation. *Clinical Risk* 5(5):168-172

Alastair Scotland
Chairman, Clinical Disputes Forum

239

THE DRAFT GUIDELINES

1. Purpose of the Guidelines

To provide guidance for lawyers and experts to arrange discussions between the experts in clinical negligence cases within the ambit of Part 35.

2. Application of the Guidelines

The court may direct a discussion between the experts in accordance with part 35.12 of the Civil Procedure Rules (CPR), alternatively there may be a discussion by consent between the parties; in each case the guidelines apply.

3. Time for Expert Discussion

(1)   The court has power to direct that a discussion be held at any stage of the proceedings. This will usually be after exchange of experts' reports.

(2)   Discussions may take place by agreement at any time including before proceedings are commenced provided that the issues have been sufficiently identified to justify discussions.

4. Purpose of Expert Discussions

The purpose of expert discussion is to identify

(1)   the extent of the agreement between the experts;

(2)   the points of disagreement and the reasons for disagreement;

(3)   action, if any, which may be taken to resolve the outstanding points of disagreement;

(4)   any further material questions not raised in the agenda and the extent to which those issues may be agreed.

5.   Arrangements for Expert Discussions

(1)   The Agenda

There must be a detailed agenda. Unless the parties agree otherwise the agenda should be prepared by the claimant's lawyers (with expert assistance) and supplemented by the defendants' lawyers, if so advised, and mutually agreed. The agenda should consist as far as possible of closed questions, that is questions which can be answered "yes" or "no". The questions should be clearly stated and relate directly to the legal and factual issues in the case.

(2)   The nature of the discussion

The discussion should take place face to face or by video link. Exceptionally, and having regard to proportionality, the discussion may take place by telephone. Save in exceptional circumstances these guidelines (and in particular paragraph 6 below) should apply whatever the form of the discussion.

It is usually advisable to have separate agenda and discussions between experts in different disciplines.

(3)   The experts should be provided with the following documents before the discussion:

(a) the medical records.

(b) If proceedings have been issued, the statements of case, the claimant's chronology, the defendants' comments on the chronology, the witness statements and the experts' reports as exchanged.

(c) If proceedings have not been issued then the parties should agree a chronology and provide this to the experts with witness statements and such experts' opinion as has been exchanged.

(4)   Unless the lawyers for all parties agree or the court orders otherwise lawyers for all parties will attend the discussions of experts. If lawyers do attend such discussions they should not normally intervene save to answer questions put to them by the experts or advise them on the law.

241

(5)   Timing

> (a) A draft agenda should be served on the defendants' lawyers for comments 28 days before the agreed date for the expert discussion. The defendants should, within 14 days of receipt, agree the agenda or propose amendments and
>
> (b) 7 days thereafter the claimant's lawyers shall agree the agenda. If in exceptional circumstances agreement cannot be reached, the parties should apply to the court.

6.   Conclusion of the Discussion

(A)   At the conclusion of a face to face discussion a statement must be prepared setting out:

> (1) A list of the agreed answers to the questions in the agenda.
>
> (2) A list of the questions which have not been agreed.
>
> (3) Where possible a summary of the reasons for non agreement.
>
> (4) An account of any agreed action which needs to be taken to resolve the outstanding questions in (2) above.
>
> (5) A list of any further material questions identified by the experts, not in the agenda, and the extent to which they are agreed or alternatively, the action (if any) which needs to be taken to resolve these further outstanding questions
>
> Individual copies of this statement must be signed by all the experts before leaving any face to face meeting.

(B)   Before the conclusion of a discussion at a distance, identical statements setting out all the information required in paragraph (A) above must be prepared and signed by each expert. Unaltered signed copies must be exchanged immediately.

7.   The experts' duty is to the Court and those instructing experts must not give and no expert should accept instructions not to agree any item on the Agenda.

Working Party

Chairman   Roger V Clements. (Obstetrician & Gynaecologist)

Lord Justice Clarke

Mr Justice Bell

Adrian Whitfield QC

David Mason (Partner, Capsticks)

Paul McNeil (Partner, Field Fisher Waterhouse)

Dr. Roy Palmer (Barrister, Medical Protection Society)

Mary Menjou (NHS Litigation Authoirity)

Arnold Simanowitz (Action for the Victims of Medical Accidents)

Professor Robert Bluglass (Psychiatrist)

Michael Collins (Dentist)

Dr Frances Cranfield (General Practitioner)

Nigel Harris (Orthopaedic Surgeon)

Dr Ben Lloyd (Paediatrician)

THE ATTENDANCE OF LAWYERS AT EXPERTS' DISCUSSIONS

Explanatory note by Adrian Whitfield QC

1. The Working Party has continued to debate the question of whether lawyers should attend discussions by experts under Part 35 of the Civil Procedure Rules.

2. We have been led to believe that judicial opposition has been expressed to the suggestion that they should, and are aware that the Blom-Cooper Working Party's Draft Code of Guidance for Experts proposes that:

    "lawyers for the parties will not normally be present at such discussions unless the experts so request."

3. In our early meetings we were influenced by the reported judicial attitude, and in any event many of us were sympathetic to it. However, we believe that our task is to produce our own recommendations, based on our collective experience. Further reflection, but in particular submissions which we have received together with our own accumulating experience of experts' meetings, have produced greater sympathy for the view that in many (if not all) cases the attendance of lawyers may be valuable.

4. Those who act for claimants have repeatedly stressed the extent of exclusion and alienation from the process of dispute resolution which their clients would feel if experts met and resolved issues without even the lawyers being present. This may not be determinative, but it is important.

5. It is convenient to return to the final "Access to Justice" report. In it, Lord Woolf accepted that in medical negligence cases

    "the suspicion between the parties is more intense": Chapter 15, paragraph 2(e)

    In Chapter 15, paragraph 68, he continued:
    "many claimants still feel strongly that the system is weighted against them, and in particular that professional solidarity among doctors is a barrier to justice for ordinary people. Whether or not this feeling is always justified, I have no doubt that it is encouraged by the lack of openness between parties which still prevails in this area of litigation."

Thus, Lord Woolf accepts as genuine the special concerns felt by medical litigants, concerns so strong that at least one of our consultees considers that the meeting of experts without lawyers being present would be in breach of Article 6 of ECHR.

6.   It is also relevant to recall recommendation 38 of Lord Woolf's final report that:

> "the case management conference should be attended by a solicitor with responsibility for the conduct of the case and at the pre-trial review the Counsel or Solicitor instructed to attend the trial must appear; the lay client, or someone fully authorised to act on his behalf, will be required to attend both hearings."

In most medical negligence cases an effective experts' discussion will be more determinative of the outcome than any case management conference. It may thus reasonably be suggested that the case for legal representation at an experts' discussion is as strong as the case for the lay client's presence or representation at a case management conference.

7.   Lord Woolf did not go so far. Although he recognised the problems, his conclusion was:

> "in the majority of cases I can see no reason why the experts should not meet alone, but I accept that there are circumstances in which this will not be appropriate:" Chapter 13, paragraph 50.

Nevertheless, he left the door open.

8.   As we understand it, there are three main objections to the attendance of lawyers at such discussions:

❖   that they will influence the experts

❖   that it will run up costs

❖   that they will not achieve anything by their attendance.

245

9. The first objection can be dismissed for a number of reasons.

❖ Legal aid franchising of claimants' solicitors and selection by paymasters of defendants' solicitors has screened out most who are unsuitable, and those who are left are working well together.

❖ A good lawyer knows that if he tries to influence his experts in the presence of his opponent he will merely be seen to devalue them.

❖ Any such attempt would in any event be noted by the opposing lawyer.

❖ Experts are becoming increasingly conscious of their duty to the Court.

❖ Such evidence of "undue influence" as we have come across is of influence by one expert of another, a point to which we shall return.

10. The questions of cost and usefulness really go together: will the attendance of lawyers be "worth it"?

11. The submissions which we have received report a number of unhappy experiences of meetings of experts unattended by lawyers. A report of case conferences during the process when the Ombudsman decides to investigate complaints includes the following accounts.

❖ "Doctors have failed to apply the correct legal test: reasonableness and not cutting edge stuff, i.e. Bolam as opposed to gold standard".

❖ "There is often quite a lot of jockeying for position ... personal relationships are not always at their easiest ... there is often bullying of less robust experts by those who are more over-bearing ... senior doctors are intensely competitive ..."

❖ "Inevitably, unexpected points are raised."

12. Litigation solicitors report exactly the same problems.

❖ "There are many accounts of experts making important errors ... of misunderstanding the test based on the balance of probability".

❖ "There are reports of certain defence experts using "political muscle" to influence decisions: the whisper "remember your duty" (to your profession) has been reported."

❖ We have had accounts of experts inviting lawyers to attend meetings to ensure documents were available and to identify them: because a previous experts' meeting had been hostile and unproductive: to keep a note to enable the discussion to proceed more freely: to advise on the interlocking of legal and medical issues.

❖ In one case a defence expert at a meeting unattended by lawyers produced a letter from a clinician in the defendants' hospital detailing a practice similar to that being debated. This document, which was selective, had never been produced before, and was used in an attempt to force a concession from the claimant's expert.

13. It is to be remembered that under the Civil Procedure Rules the record of the experts' discussion will include a statement of the issues on what they agree or disagree, and a summary of reasons for disagreement, but

> "the content of the discussion between the experts shall not be referred to at the trial unless the parties agree."

In practice, this means that there will be a limited record only made by the experts of the general debate. However, as one submission partly put it,

> "it is the lawyer's understanding of the discussion that leads to settlement or shortening of the trial."

This is a significant point. Attendance at the discussion between experts will give lawyers their best chance before trial to estimate whether the arguments of their own expert are as cogent as they had been led to believe.

14. It is not possible for us to say whether, numerically, most cases are best left to the experts alone, as Lord Woolf suggested. However,

❖ The maintenance of clients' confidence

❖ The opportunity to assist experts on the law and the facts

247

❖ The deterrent effect of lawyers' presence on inappropriate discussions

❖ The opportunity to assess the real effect of expert debate

are all advantages which may justify the attendance of lawyers at experts' discussions.

15. Unlike the Blom-Cooper Working Party, we do not consider that experts themselves should have the final say as to whether lawyers should attend their discussions. This is because experts may not, before a meeting, have applied their minds to all relevant factors, and also because experts may disagree, for example because one "powerful" expert wishes to see his opposite number alone. We believe that the decision can best be taken by lawyers (who will no doubt have consulted their experts first) subject to Court control in the event of disagreement.

16. In drafting a suggested rule it seemed important

❖ to set out a clear prima facie principle as to whether lawyers should or should not attend, in order to minimize argument between them

❖ to give the Court ultimate control in the event of a disagreement or an unreasonable agreement between lawyers

❖ to make it plain that lawyers should not normally intervene in experts' discussions

❖ to define the circumstances in which intervention was useful.

Our conclusion was that the 'default' position should be that lawyers should attend. We reached that conclusion primarily because of the importance of experts' discussions not only in the minds of litigants but also as a means of resolving cases. Against the extra cost of lawyers' attendance should be set the value of avoiding inconclusive meetings and in particular that of the lawyers' understanding of the expert issues. However, this 'default' position must be subject to Court control.

We felt it important to make it plain that lawyers should be able to answer questions, and could and should intervene if the experts seemed to be applying the wrong legal test. However we decided not to encourage them to intervene on factual issues, so as to avoid the stifling of expert debate.

After discussion, we modified the proposal that the lawyers should only answer questions and advise on the law by suggest merely that they should 'not normally' intervene in other circumstance, believing that they can be trusted to understand and not abuse the adverb.

Thus we came to suggest that the rule should be in the following form:

Unless the lawyers for all parties agree or the Court orders otherwise lawyers for all parties will attend the discussions of experts. If lawyers do attend such discussions they should not normally intervene save to answer questions put to them by the experts or advise them on the law.

17. We also suggest that the Code should include an explanatory note in the following terms:

In considering whether lawyers should attend the discussion of experts regard should be had to the following considerations:

❖ The importance of the case to the parties.

❖ The factual complexity of the case and in particular the extent to which the lawyers will benefit in their understanding of the issues by hearing the experts' discussion.

❖ The number, discipline and status of experts taking part in the discussion.

❖ The extent to which legal issues are relevant to expert discussion.

❖ The proportion between costs likely to be incurred by such attendance and the apparent size of the claim.

Revised 26.4.2000

Reproduced with the kind permission of the Clinical Disputes Forum.
Clinical Risk 2000; 6(4): 149-152.

A p p e n d i x V

Companies providing lists of Expert Witnesses

This is a list of companies known to the authors who keep Expert Registers or Panels of Expert Witnesses, or act as medico-legal agencies instructing expert witnesses on behalf of solicitors in order to obtain the report. It is not a complete and comprehensive list, but the reader who is interested in becoming an Expert Witness may find it helpful to contact these or similar companies, which are listed in an alphabetical order :-

DLA
Victoria Square House
Victoria Square
Birmingham
B2 4DL

Tel: 0121 262 5941
Fax: 0121 262 5789
www.dla.com

Expert Reports Limited
Suite C,
Canon Newton House
Evesham Walk
Redditch, Worcs
B97 4HA

Tel: 08700 751 751
Fax: 08700 752 752
E-mail: admin@expert-reports.com
www.expert-reports.com

Expert Witness
Advertising representation:
Gainsborough House
109 Portland Street
Manchester
M1 6DN

Tel: 0161 279 1000
Fax: 0161 279 1009
Email: manmed@easynet.co.uk
www.expertwitness.co.uk

IMS Global Services Ltd
359 Lower Richmond Road
Richmond
Surrey
TW9 4NZ

Tel: 01181 408 7600
Fax: 01181 408 7676

Independent Medical (UK) Ltd
Cooper House
316 Regents Park Road
Finchley
London
N3 2GP

Tel: 020 8346 8686
Fax: 020 8346 8680
Email: iml@independentmedical.com
www.independentmedical.com

Medico-Legal Reporting
2-12 Whitchurch Road
Pangbourne
Berkshire
RG8 7BP

Tel: 01189 842710
Fax: 01189 841045

Mobile Doctors Limited
4, Bourne Court
Southend Road
Woodford Green
Essex
IG8 8HD

Tel: 020 8551 8360
Fax: 020 8551 8576

PAL Medical Services Ltd
3 Harman Close
Harman Drive
London
NW2 2EA

Tel: 020 8208 9999
Fax: 020 8208 9990
Email: info@palmedical.net

Personal Litigation
freethcartwright solicitors
NEM House
34-44 Bridlesmith Gate
Nottingham
NG1 2GQ

Tel: 0115 9369369
Fax: 0115 9369352
www.freethcartwright.co.uk

UK Medical Specialists Ltd
Station House
Station Court
New Hall Hey Road
Rawtenstall
Rossendale
Lancashire
B4 6AJ

Tel: 01706 830390
Fax: 01706 830604

UK Register of Expert Witnesses
Published by
J S Publications
PO Box 505
Newmarket
Suffolk
CB8 7TF

Tel: 01638 561590
Fax: 01638 560924
Email: expert_witness@compuserve.com